LIVING WITH A WILLY

THE INSIDE STORY

Nick Fisher is an author, journalist and
BAFTA-winning screenwriter. He has
worked for many years as an agony
uncle for a number of magazines and
TV shows as well as presenting his own
programmes about his passion, fishing
and fish cookery. He lives in
Dorset with his
children — three

Contents

The Winkle Years

Growing up with a willy nestling down your boxer shorts is a strange business. Some days it's a major hoot. Other days it's a prime source of serious depression.

The early years are no problem — so long as you quickly gain a firm respect for zip fasteners. Your mum calls it your 'winkle', your granny sometimes points it for you when you have a 'tinkle' in the toilet round at her house, and everyone thinks that you and it are really very cute. Sometimes when you're out shopping with your mum, or down at the beach, or even perched on the hard shoulder of a motorway and you get caught short, your mum'll just drop your pants, aim your winkle and you get to wee where you stand.

And if passers-by see you having a wee-wee, even catch a glimpse of your tiny tackle, they just smile warmly and nudge each other. The sight of a tousle-haired tot with his tiny trousers round his ankles is a cute, funny image. In fact, it's thought to be so cute you can even buy naff little china figures of small boys taking a leak.

LIVING with a WILLY

But fifteen years later, imagine trying it again; if you got your knob out for a slash down the shopping precinct, you'd find yourself in bigger trouble than you ever dreamed. No sooner would have you pointed Percy than the police would pounce on you, throw you in a cell and charge you with indecent exposure. You'd be labelled a monster, hated by society and plastered with super-ASBOs. But it's the same winkle. Same function. Society just doesn't see it the same way any more.

Suddenly your funny sausage has become a dirty, evil symbol of sex and depravity. It's a strange business. The first few years of living with a willy are a great laugh. You can prod it with your Lego blocks and it looks all squidgy and feels funny. As you get bigger, you can use it to write your name in yellow wee on crisp white snow. You can show it to your friends and have competitions to see who can pee the highest up a wall.

But then it all starts to get complicated. Puberty comes along and the cheeky little chipolata starts to get a bit bigger and hair starts to grow round it — although for most boys, neither the hair extensions nor the size-increase happen fast enough or big enough.

Instead of showing it to all your mates and using it to put out bonfires, suddenly you get all coy and serious about it. You don't let your mum see it any more. If your gran tried to point it for you, you'd die. And having naked showers at school after games pretty much stops altogether. Boys start to shower in their football shorts or, more often, not at all. They just drench themselves in Lynx instead. All because what's inside their shorts has started to affect what's inside their heads. All because, instead of having identical trouser tackle, boys have each started to develop at alarmingly different rates. And those who feel they might be being left behind in the hair-and-girth stakes become shy about being seen to be lacking. Meanwhile those who are progressing at a pace might even start to become a bit showy-offy about what they're packing. And they're the ones who let their towel drop 'accidentally' or else do hip-shaking, todger-waggling dances around the changing rooms, just to make absolutely sure everyone knows that puberty has arrived and brought them a new set of big boys' toys.

Some lads do seem to have grown huge hefty members as fat as your arm surrounded by great tufts of thick curly hair, while others still have the pink-winkle and bum-fluff kit. Nature can be very cruel.

All of a sudden the thing that gave you so many rib-tickling childish laughs weeing up the back of the Portakabin at school is causing you a lot of grief. It's making you embarrassed about its dimension and developmental progress. It's causing you to sleep badly and worry about your normality.

And then, if all that's not enough, it starts to lead a life of its own. When you reach puberty, 'Stiffy' might as well be your middle name. You only have to sneeze and you get an erection. Even flossing your teeth can cause a major bulge in the boxers. You sit on a bus – you get a hard-on. You watch telly – you get a hard-on. You think of girls – you get a hard-on. You think of *Geography* – you get a hard-on. There is no rhyme or reason to it.

Anything can give you a stiffy.

Rather than being proud and pleased that the tackle all performs correctly, if a little too frequently, instead you get all paranoid. What if someone sees your bulge? What if they realize you've got a hard-on? The prospect suddenly seems totally horrifying. It feels as if, without a shadow of a doubt, having your unwanted erection noticed by anyone would signify the end of the world as we know it. You would be made into a social leper and outcast until the day you die. You would probably make headline news in several national newspapers and the local TV news. SCHOOLBOY GETS STIFFY, they would shout. Shock horror probe. In fact BBC2 and Channel 4 would probably make social documentaries about you.

Well actually they wouldn't. But that's what it *feels* like.

And no one understands. Girls don't understand. To you it seems their puberty worries are totally the other way round. They're only concerned with things not showing enough. They want their breasts to be larger and more prominent. You might want a bigger knob, but you certainly don't want it to show more.

The whole shame and taboo stuff that's begun to form around your penis and its unpredictable ways means that you don't ever talk about it. To anyone. You keep it secret, and so it worries you even more. But then, who would you talk about it to? Your mates will only laugh and then use your fears and confessions as ammunition for taking the mickey at a later date. Your mum wouldn't understand, and your dad's not easy to talk to, especially not about such a tender subject. So instead you just worry in silence.

After puberty's had its wicked way, and left you all bruised and confused, then adulthood and Performance Fear grabs you by the balls. Although legally you're adult enough to have sex at sixteen, you may well feel that you're not yet ready to share your willy for quite a while longer. When you get to being an adult, gone are those days of childish fun and yellow snow. Now you're being exposed to magazine articles and Internet websites that discuss stuff about sex 'technique' and 'giving your partner multiple orgasms'. Now the winkle that was there just for your very own amusement and entertainment has been mysteriously transformed into this highly complicated sex tool, which you're suddenly meant to know how to share and use in clever and difficult ways – but which came without an operator's manual. (Not that you'd read it anyway.) So, at this point in your teenage life, while you're just getting over the turmoil that puberty and your peers' teasing and preening caused you, the idea of introducing your paranoid penis to a member of the opposite sex feels like a truly major step to take, no matter how close or confident your relationship may be. Because the idea of exposing the part of you that has become so entangled in confusion and self-doubt, to another, to someone who might judge you because of it, is quite understandably seriously scary.

And it's not just the showing or the sharing of such a tender member that's the problem. It's all the expectation and macho-man baggage that comes with it. After all this doubt around puberty and your tackle, suddenly you're supposed to know just how to use it to give maximum pleasure to a girlfriend! And if you don't achieve this rather ridiculous expectation, then by all accounts you're not a 'real man'. All of a sudden you've been landed with a whole heap of new willy worries. It's not just: 'When's it going to go stiff?' 'Will anyone see it?' and 'Is it big enough to hold its own in the communal showers?' – now it's: 'Do I know how to use it expertly?' 'Will it perform as it's supposed to?' and 'Will she be sexually satisfied?' or 'Am I destined to be a forty-year-old virgin or the laughing stock of locker rooms the length and breadth of the land?'

Living with a willy is not easy. It's a funny little stump stuck in the most impractical place and built to a completely nutty design. When it's cold it feels like a whelk sitting on two dried prunes, and when it's warm it's like a limp boiled crab stick leaning against a pair of eggs in a velvet pouch.

Love it or hate it, you're stuck with it. There's nothing you can do to change it, exchange it, modify or improve it. All you can really hope to do is try and learn to love it.

Willy Worries

Is it *big* enough?

The Number One worry when it comes to the willy is size. Of all the problem letters I've received for the agony columns I've written, fears about having a penis that is too small outweigh other fears by a ratio of about twenty to one. Men and boys of all ages are totally convinced that their dicks are too small.

Usually, what they think this means is that they'll be ridiculed by their mates, rejected by women and generally destined to a life of loneliness and sorrow. It's truly amazing just how much importance can be invested in such a silly tuft of flesh.

But the truth is, boys do worry themselves into a right old state over their vital statistics. Some particularly get anxious when they find out what other boys have got.

'When I'm in the changing room at school or the swimming pool, I'm constantly, secretly looking at other boys' penises. I look because mine is relatively small and I'm sure other boys'

LIVING with a WILLY

penises are larger than mine.'

Josh (13)

'I have measured my penis a number of times with a ruler and I compared it with the average statistics. I am fifteen, but my penis only falls into the average category for a twelve-year-old. I don't want to have sex yet but I'm getting very worried that I won't be able to when I get older.'

Matt (15)

A lot of penis anxiety can be generated in the privacy of your own bedroom with a clear plastic ruler and a screwed-up impression of how long you think the 'average' penis size is supposed to be. In fact, regularly measuring your willy has got to be one of the easiest ways of worrying and depressing yourself. Although, perhaps comparing yours to someone else's is even worse.

'I am a twelve-year-old who is afraid of being abnormal. My friend can get an erection without doing anything. We also measured each other's penis and his is 2 cm bigger than mine. I want to know if I have a problem. I'm too embarrassed to go to a doctor or ask my mum.'

Justin (12)

'I am seventeen. My penis is only 8 cm long. My friends' penises all look bigger than mine. One night when I was at a friend's house his diary was

Willy Worries

open and I noticed he had written the length of his penis every month. His penis is 14 cm long. Is there something wrong with me?'

Greg (17)

Comparing your penis size with another boy's penis size is such a pointless exercise. If yours is bigger are you going to feel better about yourself? And if it's smaller, where does that leave you? Penis size is not like test scores. If you do badly one week, you can't suddenly put in a lot more effort and do well the next. What you've got is what you've got. There's nothing you can do about it. Nothing you can change. Except your attitude towards this rather absurd idea, that somehow size matters.

Sadly, rather than just dealing with their own private concerns, some boys seem to take delight in fuelling and feeding each other's fears instead. Maybe this is done as some sort of clever diversionary tactic: if you can make some other boy feel worried sick about the size of their trouser stick, then maybe you don't have to worry so much about your own.

'I'm thirteen years old. I have a small penis and no pubic hair, but all my friends have. When we have showers I am the only one who keeps my pants on, so they call me "Maggot" and they tell all the girls. Now I have no friends. I am so depressed I want to kill myself.'

Matthew (13)

9

LIVING WITH A WILLY

'I am fifteen and I have an embarrassing problem:
my penis is too small and I have no pubic hair.
Even my so-called friends laugh at me. Sometimes I
wonder if life is worth living.'

Nicholas (15)

'I am a wimp with a 12 cm willy. I get teased and
stripped in class and in PE. The teacher knows
but doesn't do anything to help. You are my last
resort.'

Very depressed

'I'm thirteen and I get teased a lot because
my penis is very small. When my class has PE,
everyone points and teases me. Now all the girls in
my class know as well.'

Alex (13)

It's obviously a pretty horrible experience being teased
by your mates about the supposedly small size of your
penis. For some boys it feels so bad they think life's not
worth living. But what's considered even worse than your
mates making fun of your dimensions is when girls get
to know about it too.

One massive worry I've read about time and time
again in letters is that your mates will take the mickey
out of your penis size so much that the girls will then
find out about it and laugh at you as well. It's such a
cruel society to live in where you have to fear being
made fun of about something that is totally out of your
control, and totally irrelevant anyway. And, strangely

enough, it works the opposite way round too, where boys worry that girls will find out first about their imagined inadequacies, and then tell all their mates.

> 'I'm a nineteen-year-old man and my penis is only 4.5 cm big. I get really embarrassed when my friends boast about how big their penises are as mine is only small. When they ask me how big mine is I lie. I have been asked to have sexual intercourse by my girlfriend. But I'm too frightened to have sex in case she laughs and tells everyone about my penis.'
>
> Depressed

In fact, girls seem to get blamed a lot for making boys feel embarrassed and insecure about their tackle. Letters often arrive from boys who claim to have been rejected by girls because they've got what the girl in question thought was a weeny willy.

> 'I am eighteen and had a major setback recently. I met this girl on holiday in Corfu. Everything went well until the last night, when she asked me to have sex with her. As we stripped she saw my penis. She laughed out loud and then went back to her room. I felt rejected because my penis isn't up to standard.'
>
> James

> 'I am seventeen and I had a sixteen-year-old girlfriend until I had sex with her. We said we

loved each other and decided to go for it. The day after, she finished with me; she began to call me Pee Wee and told everyone I had a small penis.'

Distressed

'I am a nineteen-year-old student on the verge of suicide due to an extremely embarrassing problem, which is the very slow growth of my penis. I have been recently dumped by my girlfriend due to the fact that I was a total flop in bed. When I measured it last, it was 9 cm maximum.'

Anon

'I am sixteen. I first found out I had a problem when a girl I'd been going out with offered to sleep with me. When I undressed she took one look at me and laughed. She refused to have sex with me. Then shortly after, she ended our relationship and told the whole school.'

Anon

And there are also letters from boys who are so insecure about their tackle that they even harbour future worries concerning girls they've met, or might meet one day. Girls who they're convinced will reject them, should it become obvious that their equipment's not up to scratch. Most of these letters are about a *fear* of being rejected for being too small. Many claim to be too scared to even make any advances, let alone follow through to sex, because they're convinced they will be rejected.

Willy Worries

'I am sixteen and still a virgin. I'm the only virgin in my class. The reason for this is my penis is relatively small. I have had the chance to lose my virginity twice, but am far too embarrassed about my penis.'

Tom

'I'm worried about the size of my manhood. I'm thirteen and going out with a girl who wants to begin touching me, but I'm scared she will dump me when she sees the size of my penis. I know she has been out with boys of sixteen, so they will have been bigger than me. Are there any tablets I can get to improve size?'

Michael

'I've got a steady girlfriend and we're ready to sleep together (we are both sixteen). We have thought about it very carefully and decided it's the right thing to do. The only thing is we have never seen each other naked before and my penis is not all that big. I'm worried that when she sees my penis she won't want to make love with me any more.'

Anon

The throbbing vein of inadequacy runs so deep in some boys that they're sexually paralysed through fear of what will happen if a member of the opposite sex actually sees their member. Which, in fact, is probably quite a good thing. This fear and lack of confidence may feel like an unnatural block to a natural sexual development, but I think this sort of self-limiting lack of self-confidence prevents boys, and girls, from having sexual encounters too young, and making embarrassing and regretful mistakes. All the same, boys do continually blame girls for making them scared about not measuring up to expectations. But at the same time, the paranoia of penis size is so powerful that some boys need very little encouragement to feel anxious. In fact, they don't need to have been told anything by girls – they can feel scared all on their own without any evidence to support their fear.

> 'I am seventeen. For the last year my penis doesn't seem to be getting any larger. Although I put myself about with girls, they don't say anything to my face, but I'm sure they do have a laugh at me in the local pub.'
>
> Danny

> 'I'm sixteen and my penis has not grown to the size I expected. I'm worried about going out with girls in case we get around to sexual contact and they find out about my problem. I would then become the laughing stock of the town.'
>
> Alan

Even things like television programmes, designed to put people's minds at rest, can have the opposite affect on a boy if there's already a seed of doubt sown in his head

Willy Worries

regarding his penis dimensions.

> 'My worry is concerned with condoms. My fear is
> that when I try to put one on, it will slip off. I am
> fifteen and, when fully erect, my penis measures
> 14 cm from top to bottom. I worry about this
> all the time and my worry was intensified after
> watching a programme about AIDS, which
> showed a condom being put on an enormous
> model penis.'
>
> Anon

I've often heard boys express concern about penis
size after watching documentaries, or even after sex-
education classes during PSHE (Personal, Social and
Health Education). The concern mostly revolves around
the size of the models that some sex educators use to
illustrate how to fit a condom. This is how fragile the
male ego is. Even inaccurate plastic replicas of male
penises can make us feel inadequate!

The whole issue about penis size seems to be directly
connected with self-esteem. The screwy thinking goes
that if a boy's got a big willy then he can feel big about
himself. But, conversely, if he thinks he's got a small one
then he will feel ashamed, inadequate and inferior. And
all these fears are not just sex-based – they're connected
to his status and reputation amongst his peer group too.
Having a tiny dick is somehow regarded as just about
the worst thing possibly imaginable. The ultimate fear
being that having a minute member will get you laughed

at by your mates and eternally rejected by women. So having a tiny member in the deepest and most twisted realms of macho philosophy equates to being a social outcast.

It seems truly bizarre that such a small organ can have such a monumental effect. No other part of a boy's body is steeped in such legendary importance. Not even the human brain – the biggest, most incredible, most complex, most evolved organ on the face of this earth; the very thing that controls and kicks off every single move we take and thought we make – compares to the todger. The brain doesn't get a fraction of the worry spent on it that the simple floppy flap that dangles between a boy's thighs does.

In all the letters I've answered from boys, I must have had a couple of thousand just relating to the fear connected with the possibility of having a small penis. But I can't remember receiving even one single letter in which the writer worried about having an undersized brain or an inadequately sized IQ.

Girls' view of the willy

As so many boys seem to get in a major tizz about the size of their todger and what girls' reactions to it will be, it seems only fair to let the girls have their say. After publishing one letter from a boy who was deeply depressed about his dimensions, I encouraged girls to

Willy Worries

write in and explain what they feel about boys who think they're lacking in the trouser department.

'We are three sixteen-year-old girls who all think this is a silly thing to worry about. We hope we speak for the majority of girls when we say it doesn't matter about penis size. All of us would rather go with a bloke who didn't brag about having a large penis.'

Ravers from Poole

'I had to laugh because I really do not think anyone is that bothered. Other girls only laugh about the names boys get called because they think it's good to have a laugh. The boys only pick on you because it makes them look like big, mature lads. But they are only insecure about themselves. Myself, I am not bothered one little bit what size it is.'

Annie (16)

'If you're looking for a decent girlfriend, she won't care what size your penis is, as it's the person inside that she'll be interested in. I hate it when boys go around bragging about the size of their penis. It seems they want to attract attention to themselves and they only have one thing on their minds anyway. If everyone had the same-sized everything, life would be boring.'

Cathy (16)

LIVING WITH A WILLY

'When I go out with boys, the size of their penis makes no difference at all. Sex is a private affair of love and trust. Not all girls worry about that sort of thing. I love a boy for him, not the size of his penis.'

Sally

'I'm a sixteen-year-old girl and personally I think the size of a boy's penis doesn't matter. As long as you get on well and love each other, things like that shouldn't make any difference. If girls do laugh at you, they're just being immature and not worth bothering about.'

Claire

'If your girlfriend really loves you, the last thing she'll be worrying about is the size of your penis.'

Beverley (17)

None of the girls who wrote in said that the boy who thought his penis was very small should be ashamed. None said that he was unacceptable, unlovable and not worthy to call himself a man. Quite the opposite – all of them told him it didn't matter, it wasn't an issue and that any boys who took the mickey were just immature tossers.

It's all so confusing. On the one hand, some of your mates are suggesting that any boy who doesn't measure up is a 'Maggot', 'Weeny' or 'Baby Bio'. Yet most girls are telling you it's really no big deal. They're saying that

Willy Worries

I just slung my cock over my shoulder and went as a petrol pump.'

Then there're T-shirts and boxer shorts with such witty slogans as: 'I've got 12 inches (30 cm) but I don't use it as a rule.'

There is, in fact, a whole mythology built up around men with big willies. Having a big one is seen as a symbol of potency and power and masculinity. Which of course means big cocks are also objects of envy and fantasy.

Teenage boys, and even grown men, often fantasize about having enormous equipment. Some even feel the need to write letters about it.

'I have a very bad problem. Whenever we have a shower after football or rugby I always have to make excuses as I'm too embarrassed to shower with other boys. This is because I have a very large penis. It is twice as big as some of my friends'. Why do I have such a large penis and will it affect my sex life? I might be too big to fit in a girl. I'm only twelve, so what will I be like when I'm older!'

Worried big boy

'Every time I have a shower after a match all the lads continually pick on me because I have a large penis. It is roughly 28 cm long! Is this normal? I don't want to confront my mum because she would want me to show her. I am very embarrassed, because some girls laugh at the huge bulge in my trousers. One girl keeps asking me out. Is she just after sex or does she genuinely like me?'

Anon

'I am a thirteen-year-old boy. My problem is the opposite to the letters you get from boys my age. My penis is too large. I am treated as an outcast because of this and no boys like me because girls find me so attractive. Showers are always very embarrassing. Is there any way I can make it smaller?'

Concerned

All the 'big' boys' fantasies seem to have the same element, which includes being seen in the showers by all their mates. And although in their fantasy it might be described as 'embarrassing' to be seen with such a big penis, the general feeling is that they assume other boys will be jealous of their tackle. And of course there's still the notion that having a big dick means that girls will automatically find you irresistible.

Another common situation is when boys have lied and kidded about their dimensions to all their mates, but somewhere along the line the plan has backfired.

'At school I am always boasting that I have the biggest penis and I never go in the showers after games, so no one knows any different. Then

recently my teacher forced me to go into the
shower because I was so muddy. Everyone started
looking at me and taking the mickey. Now I
cannot take much more. I may top myself.'

Steven (13)

'I am an upset fourteen-year-old. Rumours have
been going round school that I have a large penis
and it has helped increase my sex life. But the
other day in PE two girls looked down the leg of
my shorts and announced that I had actually got
a small penis. Now that everyone knows the first
rumours were a lie, I am being made fun of and
sniggered at by my classmates.'

Concerned of Derbyshire

The sad thing is that boys who genuinely do have bigger
than average penises don't actually think girls are going
to queue up to have sex with them. Quite the opposite.
They feel like freaks. The most common fear for them
is that having a large penis will make them sexually
unacceptable and unlovable. Their worry is that by
having an extremely large penis they'll get rejected for
being abnormal.

In reality though, even having a very large penis isn't
going to ruin your sex life. The vagina is an incredible
sex organ in its own right, which is able to contract
and expand. It isn't like an open tube that needs to be
filled. Instead, the walls of the vagina touch each other,
but are able to part when something is inserted. Or

LIVING WITH A WILLY

when something needs to come out, like a baby. The opening to the vagina is a ring of muscle which is usually small and tight, but when required it can relax enough and expand to allow a baby's head and body to pass through! This is quite a feat of expansion. So the chance of a penis ever being too big to fit inside simply doesn't exist.

No matter how big or small or achingly average your willy, wand, thing, string or ding-a-ling is, it will work. It will fit. It will basically be just about the same as every other bloke's.

But, most of all, it will still only be a small part of the whole of you. It's not your be-all and end-all. It's not who you are or what you do. It's just the same silly sausage you used to write your name with in the snow. The trick is just not to take it too seriously.

3

Tackle Trouble
when things don't seem right in the trouser department
Bendy ones

Considering that so much laddish talk and smutty
literature refers to willies that are 'ramrod erections' or
'steel-straight throbbing lengths of manhood', it might
come as a bit of a surprise to learn that most erections
are far from straight.

Nearly all of them tend to have a curvy bend upwards
and a great many also have a bit of a bend or a lean to
either side. Bendy ones are perfectly normal and make
absolutely no difference to sex, weeing, wanking or using
it as a thing to drown plastic ducks in the bath.

Not every boy knows how normal a bend can be. Bends
only show up when the penis is erect. And although most
men see far more penises in a lifetime than most women
do, the thing heterosexual blokes practically never see is
another erect penis, except ones on porn sites, and they
can be very unnerving to your average guy. Sure, you get
to see several limp ones in changing rooms and showers,
but an erect one is a whole different kettle of fish. By not
seeing other erections, men don't know what a strange
range of shapes and angles can quite naturally occur.

LIVING WITH A WILLY

And as with so many of these things, not knowing and not talking about it leads to worrying.

'I'm fifteen and I've never been out with a girl. All my friends have had sexual relationships and they are beginning to think that I am gay as I appear not to be interested in girls. But the problem is that I'm worried if I go with a girl and she finds out about the bend in my penis. I'm very self-conscious about this and worried that I'll never be capable of a sexual relationship.'

Nathan

'I'm sixteen and I've been going with this girl for a while. It began to get heavy; she's started to drop hints about having sex. I'm not scared, but it's just that I've been masturbating quite frequently for a couple of years now and my penis has got a slight lean to it. It curves to the left when erect. I just want to know if it will affect or interfere with my sex life in any way? I also want to know if I'm the only one who is like this or not.'

Anxious

Boys worry that having a bendy penis will make them sexually unacceptable or sexually incompatible. They also worry that they're a freak, and their mates'll find out and tease them. And some even worry that they've done something wrong and caused their penis to curve in a weird way. Usually they think they've done this by too much masturbating; they tend to feel a little bit guilty about that anyway.

But bends and curves are not a problem. As long as everything functions properly there's nothing to worry about. And even a penis with a very pronounced lean or bend won't feel any different to a girl during sex.

A bend too far

There is a medical condition that can affect the penis which is called Peyronie's disease, named after the French doctor who discovered it 200 years ago. This is when the curvature of the penis is very severe, making it painful when erect. The condition makes intercourse impossible, not because of the bend, but because of the real pain that comes with erection.

No one knows why Peyronie's disease occurs, but what happens is that the tissue inside the penis, which is usually spongy, gets covered in scar tissue that stops it from expanding uniformly.

Thankfully it's an extremely rare condition, and one that can sometimes be corrected with skin grafts and surgery.

Circumcision

The most common surgery to be performed on the willy is circumcision. Usually it's done to boy babies, either for religious or cultural reasons, and it's normally only done to teenage or adult penises for medical reasons.

Circumcision is a fairly simple operation that removes the foreskin – the tube of skin that loosely rolls to the end of the penis to cover the glans (the shiny helmet end). Jews, Muslims, Coptic Christians and many African tribes perform circumcisions on their young or baby boys. Traditionally, ritual religious circumcisions are carried out by an officer of that religion, or in African tribes by a senior tribal figure. In years past, these vital snips might have been made with anything from sharpened bones to a rabbi's toughened thumbnail. But these days, the operations that are carried out on babies in hospital normally use the 'Plastibell clamp' method. A thing like a thimble is put over the head of the penis and the foreskin is pulled over the top. Then another part of the device is clamped around the foreskin, eventually cutting it off. This is done without the use of anaesthetic. In a way, it's not unlike the method used by farmers to dock lambs' tails – a slow starvation of blood-flow eventually causes the blood-starved foreskin to drop off.

In some African tribes, circumcision is performed on adolescent boys as part of their coming-of-age ritual, which can prove very painful and risky. Generally speaking, if you're going to be circumcised, the earlier the procedure is performed, the better. In the Jewish religion, baby boys are ritually circumcised when they are eight days' old.

Some historians believe that circumcision began amongst the tribes of West Africa, who lopped off their foreskins not for any health or religious reasons, but as a way of physically marking members of their own tribe.

The opposite was true during the time of the ancient Greeks, when the shiny head of the penis (the glans) was considered sacred. To expose it was seen as totally rude and shocking. Yet all the Olympic athletes were expected to compete in the nude. So to avoid any embarrassment and unwanted flashing, athletes would tie their foreskin closed with a bit of string or a clasp. And even the Jews of ancient Greece who fancied their sons might make it as top athletes would purposely avoid circumcising their lads in order to enable them to do this.

The haves and the have-nots

In America circumcision became very fashionable about fifty years ago. Up to one and a half million circumcisions are carried out every year in the USA, for no reason other than that some people believe that a penis is better without a skin than with. Some of the reasons for wanting to have boys circumcised are pretty strange. I've come across websites where circumcision is recommended because they seem to think that the lack of wrinkled skin at the end makes peeing easier for boys! And they're less likely to miss the toilet. (In case you hadn't realized already, this is completely untrue.) This particular site even claimed that 'home-proud mums prefer it'. Wow! I've also read that many fathers who have been circumcised want their sons to be circumcised too – so they'll look the same as dad in the knob region. If ever there was a rubbish reason for having a circumcision, this has got to be the worst.

Mostly, circumcision is performed because it was, and maybe still is, believed (by some) that a circumcised penis is healthier and cleaner than an uncircumcised one.

The stuff that does collect under the foreskin of an uncircumcised willy is a goo called smegma. Also known as 'knob cheese', this whitish, waxy deposit can get very smelly very quickly, locked away under the warm sweaty darkness of the foreskin. And it can cause some fairly nasty bacteria to grow. But that's at its very worst. As long as you keep it clean, and pull it back and wash underneath it every day, a foreskin is a very useful thing to have.

For a while it was suggested that by being circumcised you were less likely to catch genital infections. Some people even claimed that being circumcised made you more resilient to serious conditions such as penile cancer and even the HIV virus. None of this has proved to be true. Medical research has proven that circumcision doesn't create a more healthy or less infection-prone penis. Circumcision at birth is a totally unnecessary procedure that gains nothing in the cleanliness department and might even lose you a point or two on the sensation side.

The head of a penis that still has a foreskin is slightly more sensitive to touch and sensation than one that has had its protective skin removed. The foreskin is there to protect the glans of the penis and to provide a moist atmosphere for it to inhabit. Without this protection, the exposed glans can become slightly desensitized through being in constant contact with underwear, rather than being permanently sheathed by its own outer-protective layer.

Whether you're circumcised or not, none of the so called 'issues' are worth getting too hot under the collar about. As long as you take baths and wash regularly under your foreskin, there is no reason to assume a non-circumcised willy will be more unhygienic than a circumcised one. And even if there may be a tiny difference in the amount of sensation experienced with an uncircumcised penis to a circumcised one, the difference is so personal and so subjective it's hardly worth worrying about. The most important thing is that your willy goes hard when you want it to, and does roughly what it's meant to do.

Medical reasons to give your willy a round neck and short sleeves
Older boys and men are normally only circumcised when there's a very good medical reason for doing it. Usually this is confined to two main problems, phimosis or balanitis. Balanitis is an inflammation of the skin covering the head (glans) of the penis. It is fairly common among uncircumcised boys and men and it can be caused by a number of different things, such as poor hygiene or allergies. Balanitis is usually easy to treat with a course of antibiotics, though in some cases, if the infection keeps recurring, circumcision might be an option that the doctor suggests. And, even less frequently, it might develop into a slightly more complicated form of balanitis that causes scarring to the foreskin. If that does

occur, a simple circumcision, under full anaesthetic, will solve the problem.

Phimosis is a condition in which the foreskin fits too tightly over the glans of the penis, making it sore and red when you try to pull the foreskin back over it. Having a too-tight foreskin is like trying to get a polo-necked jumper that's shrunk by two sizes off over your head. This condition obviously makes masturbating and sex very sore and difficult. It even makes pulling the skin back to have a pee very uncomfortable.

Phimosis can normally be treated successfully with antibiotics, and the normal development of the penis will put things right, but sometimes, if this doesn't work, a simple circumcision operation, which is carried out under a general anaesthetic, will cure the problem completely. And after being circumcised, everything should be back firing on all cylinders and fully operational within about two weeks.

A slightly worse version of the 'two-sizes-too-small polo-neck syndrome' is called paraphimosis. What happens here is that the foreskin is pulled back over the helmet of the penis and then gets stuck in the groove behind the swollen glans. What this does is cause the glans to swell up more and stop the foreskin shifting back to its normal position. This is a very rare condition and might require urgent treatment. However, a bit of clever circumcision surgery and you'll have a funny-looking bald-headed man for a willy, but no more nasty cramped sensations in the trouser department.

With all these knob problems, the same rule applies:

the sooner they're treated, the less trouble they are to deal with. And what is very important to understand is that medical circumcision is very rare. It is only ever used as a surgical option in as little as one per cent of patients.

In fact, circumcision itself is going out of fashion. In the UK in the 1930s, thirty-five per cent of men were circumcised. Every decade since then the numbers have dropped and now less than ten per cent of boys in Britain are circumcised, although among certain religious groups, including Jews, circumcision is still absolutely the norm, with over ninety-eight per cent of males having a snip.

Circumcision correspondence

Most of the letters I get about circumcision are from boys who have experienced some pain and tightness of the foreskin and don't know what to do, but think they should have the offending skin removed. As always, I encourage them to seek the advice of their doctor.

Strangely enough, there is the occasional boy who thinks that to be circumcised is pretty cool and will help enhance his sex life.

'This may sound really stupid but I want to get circumcised. All my older brothers are, but for some reason I'm not. I think mine looks ugly, and both my previous and present girlfriends refused to give me oral sex because of that. I was wondering if it was possible to get circumcised on the NHS.'

Duncan (18)

LIVING WITH A WILLY

But usually the letters are from boys who have been circumcised and who wish they hadn't, because they think of themselves as abnormal.

> 'When I was younger I was circumcised. I don't know why, because I'm not Jewish and I'm embarrassed to ask my parents the reason. When I was younger I thought I was deformed. It's really awful as my ex-girlfriend found out, and when we finished she told everyone. Now I can't go anywhere without people laughing and sniggering at me.'
>
> Depressed (14)

> 'I'm embarrassed. I've been circumcised. I had this done when I was seven and now I'm twelve. I've recently reached puberty, which makes things worse. At my school it's some sort of custom during showers after games lessons to parade around naked to show off what you've got or haven't got. I'm afraid that if boys see what I've got they will laugh and tease me and most of all tell girls about me having been circumcised.'
>
> Pete (12)

The fear of girls finding out about being circumcised is a very common one. So strong is this assumed image of abnormality that some boys seem to think circumcision will make them unacceptable and unlovable. They think being circumcised will spoil their chances of having a normal sex life.

Tackle Trouble

'My girlfriend keeps asking me to have sex with her but, as much as I want to, I refuse. I have a problem. I have been circumcised and if I tell her she is sure to dump me. I am desperate.'

Anon

'I am sixteen and I had a sexual relationship with my girlfriend who is nineteen. I was shocked when I discovered that the foreskin on my penis was too tight and I had to have a circumcision. I am very embarrassed because my penis looks very peculiar. My girlfriend has been pressurizing me into continuing our sexual relationship. What should I do? She doesn't know of my operation and I don't want to tell her as I think she would leave me.'

Concerned

Nothing cuts deeper into the psyche of the male mind than the knob. So important is the penis to some males that everything else gets overlooked. You could be the cleverest, funniest, most charming and approachable boy in the world, but if you allow yourself to get hung up about something to do with your dick, it can completely blow your self-confidence.

The idea that being circumcised or having a slightly smaller than average penis can totally affect girls' feelings towards you is madness. It really just isn't such a big deal and doesn't honestly seem to be a factor of importance on any girl's agenda. But boys who are locked into that prick=power=personality way of thinking can't see the truth of it. And what makes it worse is they feel they can't talk about their pricks, their fears or their problems. They can't talk to mates, because they'll reject them, or to parents, because they won't understand or will think it's unimportant, or to doctors, because they're too embarrassed.

The truth is, willies are not as big a thing as you think they are. And the more frank you are about your frankfurter or direct about your dick, the easier it is for others to help or be understanding. The more of a meal you make about your member, the more you get hung up and embarrassed about it.

So if your dick is giving you stick, don't suffer in silence. Talk about it, moan about it, wave it at a doctor. Don't just hide it down your grollies and hope it'll get better.

We've all got them, they're dead daft, but they can be a lot of fun too. Wear your plonker with pride.

The dick and the doctor

Given that such a large percentage of boys have a bit of penis obsession, always worrying about the size of it, the shape of it and its ability to function, you'd think they'd never be out of the doctor's waiting room.

In fact, considering that so many obviously consider it to be the most important treasure they possess and the ultimate key to the sexual universe, you'd think they'd

Tackle Trouble

be getting it checked out by the professionals practically every day. You'd think they'd treat it like a thoroughbred racehorse or a Formula One racing car, employing a full-time vet or a mechanic just to keep it in tip-top, highly tuned, A1 condition. You'd expect men to be total knob hypochondriacs of the first order.

The truth is that men and boys all too rarely go to the doctor for medical advice or treatment for their tackle. Even if they're suffering a lot of pain and heaps of worry.

So intense is the pride and embarrassment surrounding the penis that some males will suffer all manner of horrible pain and worry before being forced to admit what's going on.

'For about three years now I have had four lumps in my penis. They are quite near the top and they are loose under the skin. I can feel them. I am a very nervous sixteen-year-old, so I could not possibly go to the doctor. The thing is, me and my girlfriend are talking about sex. Is there a cream I could buy to clear this up?'

Concerned

The truth is that any lumps or bumps on the penis or testicles need to be shown to a doctor. It's impossible for any agony aunt or uncle to decipher or diagnose medical matters from letters. And they shouldn't be dealing with medical stuff anyway, it's strictly for the experts – in other words, doctors.

LIVING WITH A WILLY

Maybe there's something the medical profession could do to make themselves more approachable. Or maybe we males need to get real about our priorities. What's worse – feeling a tad embarrassed about showing your todger to a medic, or spending sleepless nights and aching days worrying that your beloved bazooka is about to drop off?

Even basic problems, like having a foreskin that's too tight (something that could easily be solved by a simple circumcision) are suffered in silence without consulting a doctor.

'I am fifteen. I have an embarrassing problem: I have a tight foreskin. I have known about it for two years and in this time I have not really been near a girl. At first I thought it would grow, but as time goes on I am less optimistic. What shall I do? It has shattered my confidence. I do not want to go to a doctor.'

Worried of Wales

'I am thirteen and very worried about my penis. My foreskin is very tight and I'm not able to get the tip or helmet of my penis out. A friend said it should loosen in time. I'm too scared to see a doctor. Does being overweight have anything to do with it?'

Anon

'I am fifteen. At school people brag about how far they can pull their foreskins back, saying they can get it right back to the hilt. I am worried because I can only pull it back a small way and daren't take it past the edge of my helmet for fear of not being able to get it back. Should I worry or are my schoolmates lying?'

David

Just in the same way as some people can touch their nose with their tongue or bend their thumb back to touch their wrist, so some lads' tackle does different things from other lads'. It doesn't mean it's any less efficient or fun to own.

Having a foreskin that is noticeably tighter than other boys', or worrying that yours feels tighter, is another example of how playground back-of-the-Portakabin banter doesn't help. If you've got a worry about your whanger and can talk to someone sensible about it – an uncle, father, mother, teacher, doctor or whoever – they can put your mind at rest or even get you medical help if you need it. Whereas a lot of your leery mates might just enjoy helping you to believe that you're a space alien with a freaky flapper which is only fit to get you a permanent job in a circus.

As with all penis and sex matters, having friends who brag and make up stories doesn't help, because it only makes you more nervous about telling the truth. There's no animal on the face of the earth who has the potential for being so cruel, thoughtless and unsympathetic as the teenage male, especially when herded into groups.

LIVING WITH A WILLY

So boys are often not only no help when it comes to solving each other's worries and problems, they can often make things much worse. It's totally par for the course for teenage boys to wind each other up and tease anyone who is concerned about his tackle, or who genuinely has something amiss with his todger. This understandably makes boys very wary about being vulnerable.

Warts and all

Spots, warts and moles are all very common additions to the average willy. They occur for a variety of straightforward reasons. Many are easy to deal with and in fact some you can just ignore. But nobody tells us this. Nobody takes you to one side when you're eleven and says, 'Now, seeing as you're the owner of a fine willy it's essential you know a few of the things that might go wrong in the years to come.'

I mean, even if you buy a bike, a car or a computer, you get given an owner's manual with a complete fault-finding guide and chapters of recommended remedies. Not so with the knob. Get born with one of those and it's pretty much up to you to learn how it works. Guidance is not very forthcoming.

In my opinion girls get a much better deal because a) they can get pregnant, so parents take much more care and consideration about making sure they know the ins and outs of their bodies and about contraception; and b) they have periods. Periods are significant because they mark a specific time when a girl's body starts to undergo changes. She is turning into a woman, therefore her mum, teachers, sister or whoever, knows that, if they haven't already done so, now is the right time to take her to one side and explain about what's going to happen.

Boys don't have periods. That doesn't mean their bodies don't undergo some pretty radical changes. Some amazing things *do* happen during puberty, like the development of the genitals.

As a foetus, a boy's balls are inside his body. During late pregnancy they drop into the scrotal sac. Usually they will have descended by the time the baby is born. During puberty the sac will start to hang lower, the balls get slowly bigger and the skin around them gets baggier. In time, one testicle starts to hang lower than the other – usually the left one. One testicle might grow faster than the other and seem bigger, but eventually in adulthood they'll normally equal out to the same size.

During puberty the whole trouser department goes through a complete refurbishing. Your balls get lower and bigger, your scrotum skin gets darker in colour, your penis gets thicker and more pronounced. And, of course, the whole shooting match gets hairier. It happens to different boys at different times and at different rates. There's no such thing as normal. Everyone's an individual, so rather than worrying that your tackle's not the same as the next guy's, just chill out and wait to see what develops.

Because boys' body changes are gradual and happen slowly, no adult or parent has to decide when it's a good time to sit a lad down and tell him about what to expect and what might be going to happen to his tackle. And so boys' development remains unfocused. No one has to warn them of anything, or prepare them for something dramatic like menstrual bleeding (a period) and so all too often parents and family tend to turn a blind eye to any physical development and just leave boys to 'get on with it'. Which can be a little unfair, especially if things happen that you don't expect to happen, or the other way around: things don't happen.

Is it any wonder then that we get worried?

One of the most common medical worries is spots on the tackle.

'I'm a normal fifteen-year-old boy who has a worrying problem. On one of my testicles and the underside of my penis I have got hundreds of little pimples. They are only tiny but quite numerous. They are normal-skin-coloured and don't seem disgusting or obscene. They're not scabby. Are they harmful or just natural?'

Ben

'I am fourteen and very confused. When I masturbate, which I do very often, little white pimples show up on my foreskin and penis. I'm scared that my girlfriend will see them and no longer want me. I don't want to see my doctor as he's a close family friend.'

Ian

Tackle Trouble

'I am fourteen with a very worrying problem. On my penis I have little goose-pimple-like spots that are yellowy in colour. I've had these spots for about a year. I'm too embarrassed to tell my mother or go to a doctor. It's really starting to concern me.'

Joe

Little spots and bumps that appear on the penis and balls are normally either hair follicles or sweat glands beginning to develop. They can look like a weird kind of whitish or creamy rash. Some are bigger than others, but usually there are hundreds of them.

It's easy to think that there may be something desperately wrong or you've caught some horrid disease. In fact it's just pubic hairs trying to push up through the skin, or oil and perspiration glands coming to life to do their bit.

Your perspiration glands develop as you grow through puberty and so do the oil glands. It's the production of all this oil and sweat that also gives you pimples on your face. The overproduction causes the pores to get blocked. It's a bit of a drag when developing, but we need the oil to keep our skin supple and need the sweat glands to keep us cool. It would be an even bigger drag if your face crumbled off from being dry, and every time you walked into a crowded room you fainted from the heat!

LIVING WITH A WILLY

Warts

Warts on the willy are very common. They can get together and form a cluster or there can be solitary warts, which take root and stand proud, causing their owner no end of consternation. Warts can come and go. Or they can dig in for the duration, never changing or shifting. They can appear on the foreskin, the helmet, balls, shaft or even inside the penis, down the urethra. They can be small, flat and smooth or large pink cauliflower lumps. They can even sometimes be too small to see at all. They can sting like hell or else give absolutely no sensation at all. But whatever they do, you can bet your granny's life savings they will make the wart-wearer worry.

'I am seventeen and still a virgin. I'm frightened to go out with girls because I have three black warts on my penis which are very large and very noticeable.'

Anon

'I've got an embarrassing problem. I've got a very big wart near the end of my penis. It doesn't hurt but I'm scared to tell anyone. I told my best mate and he's told his father who's a doctor. Now I feel as if I'll die if he mentions it.'

Martin

Although genital warts can be sexually transmitted, you don't have to have had sex to get them. They can grow all by themselves. They are really very easy to treat if they're shown to a doctor. Usually, external warts can be coated with a paint-on lotion that the doctor will prescribe and after a few treatments they just fall off. Otherwise they can sometimes be frozen off, burned off or even zapped with laser treatment. It all sounds much more exotic and painful than it really is. The removal of warts is not a big deal and is very, very common.

But if you don't get them dealt with, they can multiply and spread. And if you do have genital warts and you have sex, not only can you pass them on, they might also do greater harm to the partner you give them to. Certain types of genital warts have been linked to cervical cancer in women.

Keeping your tackle clean and healthy and getting it checked out by a doctor is not just important for the owner's peace of mind, it's also important for your partner if you do start having sex. Being a bit scared and embarrassed about going to the doctor is not only bad for *your* health – it could also be bad for the health of someone you love.

Things that won't go away

If you manage to persuade yourself that there's no way you can take your todger to the doctor, then you could be setting up your equipment and your sex life for serious trouble. In certain, severe cases you risk losing your tackle completely and with a lot of infections you could end up infertile and even impotent.

Sexually transmitted infections (STIs) fall into two

main categories: bacterial and viral. The bacterial ones live on the surface of the skin. They are quite easy to treat and can be cured completely. But viral ones get into the cells of the body and are very hard to get rid of. They can keep coming back. Ignoring these diseases will only allow them to get worse. The best way to deal with any sort of infection is to catch it quickly before it has time to do any lasting damage. But that means you do have to seek treatment from a doctor or visit a GUM clinic, which may be located at your local hospital. GUM stands for genito-urinary medicine and a GUM clinic specializes in STIs. So, apart from anything else, you don't have to feel shy or embarrassed about showing them your sick penis, because they specialize in sick penises and will, without a shadow of a doubt, have seen it all before. You might think it is the most embarrassing thing in the world to be seen in a GUM clinic, but there is absolutely no need to feel ashamed or bad – STIs are much more common than you think and we'd bet that quite a few people that you know have suffered from something a bit nasty 'down there' at some point in their lives. They just don't usually talk about it!

**Hoping and praying is not good treatment.
Making an appointment is.**
Unusual itching, redness, pain from peeing, coloured discharge and a nasty smell under the foreskin are all symptoms of sexually transmitted diseases. They're also things that a lot of boys have had and have chosen to ignore. Symptoms are a clue as to what's going on.

Tackle Trouble

If they're ignored, it doesn't mean the cause is going to clear up and the cause could be serious. There are a whole hamper of diseases you can get through your dick. The most common STIs that you might experience in your lifetime are: genital warts, genital herpes and chlamydia.

Chlamydia is a relatively new infection that is seriously on the increase, especially among teenage boys and girls. In fact, chlamydia is now the most commonly diagnosed STI in the UK. The main problem with chlamydia is that it's quite a subtle infection to begin with, one that doesn't come with a lot of very noticeable symptoms. Because of this, it's sometimes known as the 'silent' infection. Most boys who contract it may experience a bit of discharge from the tube at the end of their penis (the urethra) or maybe some inflammation or itching. But the symptoms are not dramatic and may not even be noticed at all. That's how people unknowingly pass the disease on. And chlamydia is very easily passed on to partners during sex or genital contact. It can cause lasting damage to girls if they catch it, affecting their reproductive system and possibly causing problems with getting pregnant and having babies in later life. If left untreated in boys, it can lead to serious infections and damage to the urethra, affecting sperm function and fertility.

The good news is that chlamydia is very easily tested for and easily treated with antibiotics. In the UK a simple and free test is available for fifteen- to twenty-four-year-olds as part of the National Chlamydia Screening Programme. The test is very quick and not at all embarrassing – you go to a clinic and take your own swab in a private cubicle or loo, so there's no need to get your tackle out. The test can be arranged easily through an STI clinic or by visiting your GP (see the website details at the back of this book for more information). It's recommended that all sexually active young people should have the test every year, and it's definitely worthwhile. Because if chlamydia is left untreated, it can cause serious harm to yourself and your future partners. And currently chlamydia is rife among teenage boys, with increases in the infection rate growing by twenty per cent each year.

Genital herpes: catch herpes and you've got it for life. Herpes is a viral infection for which there is no absolute cure. It's a long-term, unpleasant condition that you really, really don't want to catch. Herpes will initially show up as small itchy sores and blisters that appear on the penis. They will often fill with a clear liquid that turns yellow in time. And when these blisters burst, the resulting ulcer will dry up and develop a scab. All this is usually accompanied by flu-like symptoms and a general sense of irritation around the tackle. Most people who carry the virus are unaware that they've got it until they have an attack of the symptoms and sores. These irritating and painful attacks normally occur four to five times within the first two years of catching the virus and then eventually become less frequent. But herpes is affected by your general health and physical well-being too. Getting run down or sick, exposing infected areas to too much sunlight or drinking excessive amounts of alcohol can create opportunities for the virus to reawaken and the symptoms to flare up again. There is no total cure for herpes, but antiviral drugs can minimize the nastiness and frequency of the attacks. Obviously it's better not to get it in the first place. It's normally caught by having intimate sexual contact with somebody who has active herpes sores on their genitals. It can't be caught from anything else, like cups, cutlery or towel sharing. And wearing a condom will provide protection, so long as any sores are covered. It's very infectious, so if you think you or your partner might have it, get it checked immediately and avoid sexual contact.

Gonorrhoea (aka the clap) is an old-fashioned infection that looked to be beaten until recently, when it started to make a strong comeback. These days it has become the second most frequently occurring STI in the UK and it is most common among young men. It's caused by a bacteria that is found in the semen or vaginal fluid of infected men or women. So it's transmitted most commonly by having sex with an infected partner without using a condom. It can also be passed between people who share the same sex toys, such as vibrators, if they haven't been properly cleaned or haven't been covered with a condom. In men the symptoms of infection usually show up within two weeks of having sex, and they may include: a yellow or white discharge from the tip of the penis; pain or irritation when peeing; a more frequent than normal need to pee; an itchy anus, which might also produce some discharge, and pain or tenderness around the balls, which might also appear a bit red and inflamed. Some men don't show any obvious symptoms at all. To be diagnosed, you will need to have a painless test that involves having a cotton-wool swab taken from your penis, anus or throat, by your doctor or at a GUM clinic. This swab is then sent to a lab for analysis. But, if gonorrhoea is left untreated, it can eventually cause painful abscesses to grow on the testicles, which may in the worst cases lead to eventually losing a testicle. And if it is transmitted to a pregnant woman, it can seriously and harmfully infect their baby. Normally, a course of antibiotics is enough to treat it successfully. Although if you do happen to contract gonorrhoea, it's important to also be tested for other infections at the same time, as a significant number of people who test positive for gonorrhoea also find they test positive for chlamydia too.

Syphilis (aka the pox): like gonorrhoea, syphilis is a sexual disease that is often associated with ancient times. However, both diseases have witnessed a very worrying comeback in recent years. Syphilis starts with one or more sores appearing on the skin, on or near the penis or vagina. These sores are called chancres and quite often they are totally painless. But the disease of syphilis is a complex one that comes in three stages: primary, secondary and tertiary. The first appearance of these sores is evidence of the primary stage. And it's contact with these same sores that causes the spread of the syphilis bacteria from one person to another. However, wearing a condom during sex doesn't necessarily remove the risk of catching the disease, as these sores might not just be present simply on the areas covered by a condom. Two to ten weeks after the sores have appeared, the secondary stage will occur. This stage can produce a range of symptoms from a skin rash and excessive tiredness to a headache and sore throat. Worryingly, all these symptoms may disappear without treatment, but the syphilis hasn't then gone away. It's quietly evolving into the third, or tertiary, stage, which is a very serious problem indeed when it re-emerges. The result of long-term infection can lead to blindness and senility. So to ignore the symptoms of syphilis and let it develop untreated is very dangerous indeed. Again, syphilis can be quickly detected by simply going to your GP or GUM clinic, where they'll take a blood sample and a swab sample for analysis. The results are normally available in around seven to ten days.

Pubic lice (aka crabs): you don't just get these little crab-like creatures from having sex with someone who already has them. You can potentially catch them from just cuddling, or possibly from bedding, clothing and towels too. These little beggars are also known as crabs, because they have a claw-like arm to help them latch on to the base of your hairs. They don't just live in pubic hair either, and will also take up residence in chest hair, beard hair, hair around your anus and even in your eyebrows or eyelashes. The way you know you've got them is that you itch like anything and you might just notice them crawling about if you look very closely or use a magnifying glass to inspect your hairy bits. Or you might spot a sprinkling of dark brown powder on your skin or in your pants. This brown powder is the lice droppings! You might also find bluish marks on the skin around your thighs or low on your tummy. These are the marks they leave after biting your skin and sucking your blood. If you don't deal with the lice quickly, they'll spread to your eyebrows, underarms and eyelashes, which will make you itch for Europe. Infestation of the eyelashes can also create sores, which may develop into more serious eye infections and could put your sight at risk.

Lice can't leap. They can only crawl. So they are normally only transmitted from close intimate physical contact. But you don't have to have sex with an infected person to contract your own personal lice population, nor will wearing a condom make any difference. To stop the irritating itch, a trip to your doctor, a pharmacy or a GUM clinic will get you a lotion or a cream that you can apply in order to kill off the lice. Make sure you fully understand how to use the treatment you're given, as you will usually need to reapply it for a second time to make sure you terminate any new lice that might have hatched from any remaining eggs.

Tackle Trouble

Thrush: thrush isn't strictly a sexually transmitted infection. Thrush can occur in both men and women without any sexual contact taking place. Thrush is caused by a fungal bacteria that may naturally exist within your body. It might get triggered by sexual contact, but also by just being run down and overtired, or even through the use of some antibiotics. What prescribed antibiotics do is to kill off the bacteria in your body in order to help you fight infection. But most antibiotics can't discriminate between good and bad bacteria, and so they may affect the natural balance of good bacteria in your body. If this happens, it gives thrush an easy ride, because your body can't defend itself against it. Thrush bacteria occurs naturally in a woman's vagina and usually does no harm. Sometimes, though, it can multiply and cause an infection that a man can catch under his foreskin. Men can get thrush too, without having sex. The symptoms include a redness and itchiness under the foreskin on the glans, and an increase in the build up of smegma. You might even feel a stinging sensation when you pee and possibly some evidence of discharge from your penis. The correct antifungal cream can clear it up. But if it's not treated you may just go on reinfecting your partner, who'll just go on giving it back to you. It's a vicious and very itchy cycle. Personal hygiene is very important to avoid thrush. The bacteria thrives in warm, damp conditions, so make sure you wash regularly around your penis, under and over your foreskin (if you've still got one) and around your balls too. Then make sure you dry it all well.

Don't leave your tackle damp. And don't use perfumed shower gels or overly scented soaps to wash with, as the chemicals in these can irritate the skin and aggravate the thrush. Wearing loose boxers instead of tight briefs might help to keep your tackle cool and properly aired. This can also reduce the risk of encouraging any bacterial growth.

Urethritis (NSU – non-specific urethritis): NSU is a sexual infection that primarily affects men. Basically, it's an infection of the urethra, the tube which runs through the centre of your penis and which pee comes out of. If when you go for a slash it suddenly feels like you're peeing razor blades, then you might possibly have caught NSU. Any pus visible at the end of the penis is a clue too, as are aching balls or unusual pain during sex. NSU is often related to chlamydia, as if you've contracted chlamydia it might cause you to suffer from NSU as well. However, NSU isn't specifically related to any particular disease – that's why it's called 'non-specific'. It is easily treated with a course of antibiotics, but if it's ignored it might cause long-term problems with your testicles.

Jock itch: this delightfully named nasty is also known as jock rot, because it's often caught by lads who do a lot of sporty, athletic things. It's nothing to do with sex. It's a fungal infection caused by getting damp and sweaty a lot and not allowing the skin to dry out properly. It can also be caused by wearing too-tight trousers or underpants, which don't allow the air to circulate properly. It comes up as an itchy redness around the genitals. Dusting with talcum powder might be enough to stop it. Otherwise antifungal powders and creams can be bought from the chemist.

HIV (Human Immunodeficiency Virus): HIV is a sexually transmitted virus that eventually attacks the body's natural immune system. This means that the virus attacks special cells in human blood that would normally protect the body from disease and infections. With the blood cells damaged, the body is more likely to develop serious illnesses, or even fatal diseases like cancer. HIV weakens the body's natural ability to defend itself. HIV can lead to AIDS (acquired immune deficiency syndrome), which is a syndrome in which a person's immune system gives up entirely and puts them at risk of dying from contracting minor infections.

Two ways you can catch HIV are from having unprotected sex and from sharing syringe needles with an infected person. The needles can transfer the virus because they have traces of infected blood on them. Sex can transfer HIV because spunk (or semen as it's properly known), menstrual blood and vaginal fluids can all carry the virus.

Oral, anal or vaginal sex with an infected person can transfer the HIV virus. Using a condom lessens the risk. But you definitely can't get HIV from shaking hands, sharing towels, sitting on loo seats, eating off crockery or any other everyday things. The most common way that

HIV is spread is through sex. There's no way of telling if someone has the virus as it has no outward visible symptoms. The only way someone can find out if they've been infected is to get an HIV blood test at a GUM clinic or at their doctor's surgery. The earlier that the HIV virus is detected, the more effectively it can be treated. So testing early is always best. In the past some people at risk of HIV were very reluctant to be tested, because they felt there was no cure and therefore it was better not to know. Now, HIV medicines are so sophisticated that it's absolutely possible to live a normal and happy life with the virus – if it's treated early enough. So being tested early if you think there's a risk is super important. The symptoms of primary HIV infection might include a blotchy rash on your chest, persistent tiredness, night sweats, weight loss, diarrhoea, white spots on the tongue, a dry cough or a fever that lasts for a number of weeks.

There is no cure or vaccine for HIV. However, the advance in treatments means that someone who does contract the virus nowadays may live as long as someone who doesn't. The way that HIV is most commonly contracted is simply from having unprotected sex. The simple way to prevent catching the virus is always to wear a condom.

'Because you're worth it'
You may be familiar with an irritating hair advert in which a woman uses a pricey shampoo on her flowing locks and dreamily mutters 'Because I'm worth it'.

Tackle Trouble

Well, this is exactly how you should be thinking about condoms. You should use one because, quite simply, you're worth it. Your health, and the health of your partner, is precious and you shouldn't even consider jeopardizing them. Pretty much all the STIs mentioned in this chapter can be avoided, or the risk of catching them lessened, by simply wearing a condom.

And if warning signs do present themselves, do something about it. Just think of your dick as a Ferrari 430 Scuderia, which the nice people at Ferrari simply gave you for free. They also said, when they gave it to you, that you could get it mended or serviced, without any charge, whenever you wanted. All you had to do was just ring the Ferrari Freephone number and they'd sort it out for you as soon as humanly possible. Wouldn't that be fantastic?

So, you get given this totally brilliant motor. Absolutely the dog's bollocks. The business. Minted. It'll do 180 mph top whack, cruise at 105 mph and glide round corners like ice cream on a hot plate. Look after it, and this car will give you years and years of super-intense pleasure. You can even share it with people you really like, and give them pleasure with it too. Every time you use it you'll just feel a warm glow of creamy satisfaction.

That's one gift that has just got to be worth looking after – hasn't it?

Now imagine if it did go wrong. One day it starts smoking out of the exhaust and juddering when you put your foot down. Maybe one of your passengers points out that it's not sounding as smooth as it normally does or looking too perky. What would you do? Ignore it and hope it gets better on its own? Give up driving this beautiful motor for ever? Or phone the Freephone?

Of course you'd phone. They said they'd mend it. You know you'll soon be back on the motorway having a wonderful time after they've tinkered with it. So you'd phone, no question about it. Blimey, if the thing even so much as coughed you'd be round that Ferrari garage faster than a whippet with the runs, to get it sorted.

But, sadly, when it comes to looking after their penises, this fabulous organ that could supply decades of indescribably exciting pleasure, so many men just never pick up the phone or visit the garage.

Look after your willy and it'll look after you.

4

The Willy in Action

Erections

I can clearly remember, aged about four, sitting on my bedroom floor in my pyjamas, prodding my todger with a Lego block. A few prods and the little pink thing would feel funny and start to go stiff. It was a whole lot of fun and much more interesting than building Lego models. Apart from anything else, this is probably the main reason I didn't become a famous architect. Ah, if only I'd been less interested in my willy.

Early erections are strange. Although you know they feel nice, you don't really know *why* they feel nice, or what exactly is going on downstairs. There was this pole in my mum's garden that she used to tie up the washing line. As a five-year-old I would shunt up it, clamping it in my hands, between my feet and through my groin. The sensation of climbing this pole felt very nice, much nicer than any other climbing experience I ever had. I had no idea why. The fact that it rubbed against my willy as I shunted meant nothing. I didn't really connect the sensations.

Even running very fast as a pre-adolescent could

make me experience that same warm excited feeling at the bottom of my tummy. Presumably the sensation of my thighs rubbing together excited my penis. But I didn't know; didn't have a clue.

That's the thing about erections. For the first few years you live in blissful ignorance of what they are and why they happen. You just get to enjoy the occasional yummy sensations. Then you find out what they are. You learn about their sexual significance and taboo reputation, and suddenly you're thrown into a mass of embarrassment and shame every time you get one.

'I am sixteen and need help desperately. I just can't stop getting erections. I embarrassed my girlfriend in front of her parents. I just can't control it. I daren't go swimming because people will see me and laugh. My life is a complete misery. Do all boys go through this? Am I abnormal? I feel so dirty.'

Nick

'I have this terrible problem that I can't talk to anyone about as it is embarrassing. Every time I see this girl I have an erection. I can't control it. A lot of people might think I'm disgusting but I can't help myself. Please help, I'm becoming suicidal.'

Jim

'I am a boy of fourteen and three-quarters. I don't know what to do. My penis keeps becoming erect whenever it feels like it. It's got a mind of its own.

The Willy in Action

I think of something boring or a lesson but nothing
happens; it doesn't go down. I'm scared someone
will notice and I'll get embarrassed, so I have to
cover my waist with something.'

Leeds fan

The reason why an erection is embarrassing is
because it's seen as an indication of sexual goings-on.
Supposedly, the idea is that if you've got a hard-on
then you must be having sexy, and therefore naughty,
thoughts. So the embarrassment is about other people
knowing what you're thinking, particularly as it's of such
an intimate nature.

The ironic truth is that you could be thinking about
carpet tiles and still get a stiffy. If your willy has got an
urge to stand up, then it really doesn't matter what's
going on in your mind, it's going to do what it wants to
do.

It's the shame connected with erections that is such
a hard thing to accept. Every normal male experiences
a lot more erections than are required for having sex.
We all have had stiffies at times when they're definitely
not required. But even though they're an everyday
occurrence there's still a whole lot of fuss made about
them. They are very common, very natural things to
have, but they often get regarded as terrible, rude and
offensive.

It is absolutely illegal to show an erect penis on
television or in a mainstream publication. Why? You're
allowed to show naked breasts, exposed pubic mounds,

even limp willies. But as soon as they become erect, suddenly they become illegal. What's the big deal? Why does their texture make such a difference? Obviously it's because of what an erect penis represents, i.e. a male organ ready for sex.

Is it any wonder boys get embarrassed about having unwanted erections when so much fuss is being made about a straight-up todger? And, of course, it doesn't help when other people point it out.

'I'm fifteen and just about every time I get on a bus I get an erection. I went on a bus with my girlfriend into town and when she noticed she wouldn't stop laughing at me. Everybody turned round and there was I with this lump pointing up at me from my trousers. I wanted to die. Is there something wrong with me?'

Embarrassed

'I am a fourteen-year-old boy and my girlfriend was telling me a story of two people making love. As she told me I got an erection. When she noticed my erection she was cross and now thinks I'm sex mad. And she's told everyone at school and now I'm a laughing stock.'

Jason

Buses and coaches can be a nightmare in the unwanted erections department. There's something about the throb and vibration of diesel engines that can easily entice an erection. You might be totally unaware of anything,

The Willy in Action

just happily minding your own business on your way to school, and suddenly you realize you've got a stiffy.

Erections can creep up on you when you least expect them.

> '**I** am an eighteen-year-old and I'd like to know if it's normal to have erections an average of eight or nine times a day without physical stimulation? Do I have too many erections? Even when I am not thinking of sex, like when I'm sitting playing the piano during music lessons, I get erections. Is this harmful?'
>
> John

Unwanted erections can be annoying, they can be embarrassing if noticed and they can be uncomfortable. But let's not get carried away with their importance — they can also be dealt with fairly easily. Erections become most noticeable and most inconvenient when they have room to manoeuvre.

If you've got really baggy boxer shorts or loose tracksuit bottoms, then there's nothing to stop the stiffy sticking out. Some boys find it helps to wear more constricting briefs, or even two pairs of briefs when they're going through a particularly active phase in the trouser department. Wearing a jockstrap can also be an effective way of restraining a wild willy.

Hiding unwanted erections is not really that difficult, so long as you've got your clothes on. But there are times when you haven't got anything to hide what's going on. A lot of boys experience problems with over-proud penises when they are naked in communal showers.

'Please don't laugh at me. My problem started a few months ago during the rugby season at school. I was in the showers after a match, when I got an erection. Everyone started to laugh at me and called in other people to see. I ran out of the showers on the verge of tears, got depressed and ran home. When I went back to school everyone laughed at me and called me names. I am dreading the next time I have to go in the showers with other people. I don't understand how it happened. I'm sure I'm not gay. I feel so depressed I want to die.'

Anon

Instead of just being an embarrassing lump in your trousers, an erection can be an excruciatingly embarrassing reality in an all-male environment. Mainly because boys are so frightened of being thought of as gay by their peers. They're frightened because of the stick and mickey-taking they'd have to put up with.

When you think about it, getting an erection in the showers is not that surprising. If geography lessons and coach trips can get you hard, even without thinking, it's not that unlikely that warm showers will work too.

Also, whether you like it or not, being naked in among other naked bodies, even if they are your

The Willy in Action

own sex and you consider yourself heterosexual, can be a stimulating experience. Especially during your adolescent years, when your hormones are working overtime anyway, the sensation of stripping off and then getting into the shower can have an arousing effect on your penis. Even if you're completely repelled by the whole idea of naked men's bodies and communal bathing, your knob doesn't necessarily know that. We've all experienced a thousand erections at totally inappropriate times and situations. This is just another example.

Getting a stiffy in a locker-room shower doesn't mean you're gay or attracted to men's bodies. All it means is that your tackle is working well, it's doing all the things it's supposed to, but it's just doing a spot of overtime. Not a problem. Not abnormal. Just a healthy, happy horn, doing its thing.

Morning glories

There are times when you don't want an erection, like in the changing rooms or on the school bus. There are times when you do want a stiffy and you can't get one, often during your first sexual experiences. And there is one time when nearly every male gets an erection regardless: first thing in the morning .

Waking up with a stonker is very common. These

early morning erections are sometimes called 'piss-hards', because people assume that they've got something to do with the build-up of pressure in your bladder overnight. But there isn't any evidence to prove this is the case. What is much more likely is that it's simply the leftovers from the last dream you had.

When you dream, you'll often get an erection. This might happen up to five or six times a night and no one really knows why. It doesn't mean you're dreaming about sex. On the contrary, you might be having nightmares, or not remember the dreams at all, yet still your knob will stand to attention. Waking up with a stiffy might make you want to masturbate, but, strangely enough, often the first erection of the day isn't a very sensual one. And usually if you ignore it, it'll soon go limp and let you get on with life.

wet dreams

The scary thing about wet dreams is not so much that they happen, but the fact that no one bothers to warn you that they might happen.

The first time I woke up with a puddle of spunk on my pyjamas I was frankly amazed. I could see it wasn't wee, I knew it was semen, but I couldn't think how or why it was there. I had no recollection of any dream; I just woke up sticky.

Many boys between the ages of twelve and fifteen

The Willy in Action

will experience wet dreams. Some might have loads of them and some might not have any. Personally, I can only lay claim to ever having two. One I can remember was accompanied by a sexy dream; the other – nothing.

Physically speaking, all that's going on is that your sperm-producing equipment is having a bit of a test run. It's doing a quick once round the track while you're asleep. To check out the motor and make sure the spunk manufacture and distribution network is all properly in place.

It's a perfectly natural subconscious way for the body to empty your semen stores in order to start up production again. Sometimes you get an added bonus and a sexy dream to go with the clear-out and sometimes you don't.

Often boys will experience their first-ever ejaculation through a wet dream. The first time they ever come could be through this mechanism of subconscious triggering. Boys who masturbate regularly tend to have fewer wet dreams, although you can have both.

So the first time you ever come might be a complete surprise that happens in the middle of the night and leaves you to wake up to a puddle of stuff you've never seen before sticking to your sheets. To think that nobody takes the trouble to warn you about this is a bit out of order really. It could frighten the life out of you!

Lots of boys that it's happened to think they've wet themselves, or else think they've been bleeding through their dick. Some even think they've done something really terrible and that this is the punishment.

LIVING WITH A WILLY

Whether or not you have any recollection as to what the reason for you coming during the night was, the sense of embarrassment is always very strong and the practicalities of what to do about the sheets are also a big issue.

'I've been going through a phase of wet dreams, which I can't control. One morning my sister caught me trying to hide the sheets and threatened to tell our mum and dad. I don't want her to tell Mum and Dad what I'm going through.'

Confused

'I am fourteen. A few nights ago I woke up to find that my bed was damp. My mum asked me why it was wet, so I told her I had weed in it overnight. She was very cross and told me I shouldn't be doing this at my age. The truth is I don't think I did wee in my bed. Could this have been a wet dream? If so, what exactly is one and why do we have them? My friends always laugh and joke about them at school but I don't really know what they are.'

Embarrassed

Any damp patches that you find in bed in the morning that have got nothing to do with wee, are very likely to be semen. Nocturnal ejaculations of semen can't be controlled, they're not your 'fault', they're not dirty or bad or anything to be scared about. They can be a tad messy, but wearing underpants in bed if they happen a bit frequently will soon solve that problem.

Wet dreams aren't just a teen thing, although they are most likely to occur during your adolescent years. You can go on experiencing wet dreams or 'nocturnal emissions' occasionally at any stage in your life.

'I have started having wet dreams but I haven't really started puberty yet. Nobody else in my form has had a wet dream apart from me. Why is this?'

Chris (13)

'I have wet dreams occasionally but I've heard that these aren't real sperm. I'm concerned because I thought these only lasted through puberty, and now I'm seventeen.'

Luke

There are many boys who worry about having too many wet dreams.

'My problem is I keep having wet dreams. I can't help it. I usually have one every night. Is there any way I can stop them? One of my friends said that if you were having them you would run out of sperm and therefore not get a girl pregnant. When I'm married I do want a baby. Will all these wet dreams cause a problem for this?'

Lee (15)

LIVING WITH A WILLY

On the other hand, some boys are mortified that they're missing out by not having any.

> 'I know this might sound stupid but I am a seventeen-year-old lad and I have never had a wet dream. What is the cause of this? All my friends have had wet dreams but I haven't. Could this be because I am overweight?'
>
> Anon

Like everything else to do with the willy, wet dreams get confusing. Some boys go on bragging about how many wet dreams they've had and how brilliant they were, while other boys feel racked with guilt and shame and try and cover up the fact that it's happened.

In some ways you could say that wet dreams are the nearest boy equivalent to a girl's periods. If a boy has a wet dream, it might well be the first ever ejaculation he ever experiences, and so it could for him mark the start of puberty. Girls, however, get the onset of periods explained to them, by mothers, aunts, sisters, teachers, magazines and even TV adverts. What do most boys get? A sticky willy and a lot of worry.

It's the same old story. When it comes to growing up with a willy, most of the time you just have to guess and make it up as you go along. Because no one tells you anything.

The Willy in Action

Masturbation

I got taught how to wank. I had a mate called Mervyn, who was very advanced in the sex self-exploration field. And, anyway, Merv told me about this great new sport I was missing. When I voiced an interest, he obligingly showed me how to do it. Good old Merv, he set me up for life. I can't say I've looked back since. I certainly haven't stopped.

Although, I have to admit, it wasn't all plain sailing from the word go. Even though I could get a hard-on easily by a bit of fiddling and diddling, and even though I definitely enjoyed banging the old bishop, I got no end result. When Merv reached the climax of his doings, he spurted a glob of come, but not me. The well was dry. At the tender age of eleven, my testicles weren't producing any semen to create an ejaculation. This worried me. It didn't put me off beating me meat, but I wasn't quite sure why I couldn't come up with the creamy white goods like Merv.

It didn't take long before I'd forgotten I was worried, because soon enough I was churning out the old love juice and was as happy as a sandboy eagerly playing with my new toy.

Before I was shown what to do, I knew a bit about getting a stiffy, I knew what sex was, but I had no idea about wanking. Although it's a bit embarrassing to think about how I found out, thankfully I haven't seen Merv since, so it's not a big deal. But in many ways I have a lot to thank him for, because since then no one has ever talked to me about masturbation.

I had some really awful sex education at school, but the biology teacher never mentioned the old hand shandy once. Masturbation is yet another one of those secret male things that no one really talks about properly. Sure we all call each other 'wankers' as an insult and might have a laugh and joke at someone's expense about the practice of pulling the plonker. But there's never any reassurance or honest talk about what it is lads do under the privacy of their own duvet.

Luckily I grew up thinking of it as a very normal and pleasant pastime and managed to devote a huge part of my teenage time and energy to eagerly pummelling my mutton.

I was lucky. A lot of boys get very screwed up about masturbation.

'I am fourteen and I masturbate every day, sometimes twice or even three times. I have noticed my penis sometimes feels sore. Am I doing it any harm? Does this mean I'll use up my sperm and not be able to father children?'

Very worried

'I am twenty and still a virgin. I think I masturbate too much. As soon as I wake up I masturbate and then after each meal. I also masturbate when I go to bed at night. Do you think I'm abnormal?'

Ben

The Willy in Action

One of the most common worries is not so much about the act of masturbation but whether it's 'allowed' or 'healthy' to be doing it. The truth is there's no medical reason why masturbating four times a day will do you any harm. And probably most boys go through a phase of flogging the dolphin like it's going out of fashion. But usually it's just a phase and things calm down again later, then they might pick it up again for an enthusiastic spurt at another juncture. Frequency is not a real problem unless wanking becomes obsessive.

Compulsive masturbation, when you do it continually for the escapism of giving yourself constant self-pleasure, is spooky, but doing it up to three or four times a day is just youthful exuberance.

So some guys do feel guilty about fiddling with the fun rod, because they're scared about what it's doing to their bodies. Others get scared because of what it's doing to their souls.

> 'In my religion masturbation is seen as a sin. I have masturbated lots of times, but I really try hard not to. I hate myself for doing it, but I can't find it in me to resist. I must be weak and bad. I don't know who to tell.'
>
> Anon (15)

Being caught having a wank seems to be something that a lot of boys fear, and some have unfortunately experienced.

LIVING WITH A WILLY

'About two weeks ago I was getting ready to go out on a date with my girlfriend. I went into the shower and got undressed, not knowing I hadn't locked the bathroom door. I washed and turned the shower off, then had an urge to masturbate. My neighbour was downstairs chatting to my mum. When she came upstairs to use the toilet she came in and caught me masturbating.'

Embarrassed

'I am sixteen and my thirteen-year-old sister caught me masturbating in the bathroom. It was very embarrassing and now everyone in the sixth form I attend knows about it.'

Man United supporter

Knowing we all wank is one thing, but being caught in the act is another. All the same, it's not a life-or-death thing either. The moral of the tale is that you should take care where you choose to have a wank. It's something that we do in private for our own pleasure, so if you're running the risk of being caught by leaving the door unlocked, then maybe you're after extra thrills. Maybe you want to be caught. In which case you're being unfair, because then you're being an exhibitionist. You're aiming to get thrills at the expense of shocking someone else, which is well out of order.

The Willy in Action

You won't grow out of it

There's a bit of a myth that goes around which suggests tickling your pickle is only something you do when you're a teenager. The implication is that when you grow older and start having a regular 'real' sex life, then you won't need to masturbate and so you'll stop it forever. This is total, undiluted tosh. Once a wanker – always a wanker.

You might not varnish your pole quite as often when you're in a sexual relationship as you did when you were young, free and seriously single. But there's absolutely no reason to suppose that you'll give it up. Even if you're having top-class, rampant athletic sex every day of the week, it doesn't mean you won't fancy a quick J. Arthur Rank once in a while.

It's a different kettle of fish. It's something you do to relax or escape or enjoy a fantasy. So in that respect it's completely different from the sex you might have in a loving and caring relationship.

Some girls find it hard to understand how attached boys get to wonking their conker; they might even get upset and hurt by it.

'My boyfriend and I are both eighteen and have had a very active sex life. We normally make love about five or six times a week. So it comes as a bit of a shock to me to find that he still masturbates occasionally (normally on the first few days of my period, when we don't make love). He says that if he doesn't relieve himself he gets a build-up of tension. Does this mean I'm not satisfying him? Or does he have abnormal needs?'

XXX

Sex and masturbation are definitely two different things. Maybe it's because we discover masturbation in our teens and have so much fun with it that it's hard to give up. And indeed, why should we? Most men naturally go on shaking hands with Rosy Palm and her five little sisters until they basically can't get it up any more.

Wanking is good for you

Apart from being a cracking good way to pass a few minutes now and again, it can be argued that playing pocket billiards can actually be quite beneficial. During adolescence, when your hormones are working overtime and your sexual urges are going bananas, a wank can be a great comfort.

Masturbating is a good way of relieving sexual tension and frustration. Getting a grip on your dick can help you keep things in perspective and not get too worked up with sexual dissatisfaction. It's also a good way of getting to know your own sex organs. Wanking allows you to investigate your sexuality, both physically and mentally.

The way you masturbate and bring yourself to the point of orgasm puts you in touch with what you like and how you personally achieve the most exciting orgasm. This sort of information can be a lot of use during sex. If you can guide a lover to touch and caress you in the way you find exciting, then it should be exciting for them too. If you know your ins and outs, your nooks and crannies and your likes and dislikes, it all goes to help when making love.

As for your mental sexuality, the sort of things you think about while you're pulling your pudding are the things that turn you on. Exploring your fantasies in the privacy of your own head helps you understand what it is that you find most exciting and arousing. It's about understanding what makes you tick sexually.

Some boys can't be bothered to fantasize and instead they simply want to look at pictures to get themselves excited. Magazines have been the wanking fodder of men and boys since time began. And now, with the advent of internet porn, pictures of naked women and men committing all manner of sexual acts are readily available at the click of a mouse. Porn is a bit of a lazy way to get yourself excited. And, like I said before, it can give you a very warped idea about sex. The net is sadly full of really over-the-top, perverse sex. Sites that want to sell advertising or attract subscribers are often very sensationalist. These sort of sites can be very confusing. Some of the sexual images on the net that involve bizarre sexual acts are far from being normal and often far from being arousing. Looking at too much weird sexual stuff is only going to confuse you and even put you off sex, while looking at a constant parade of perfect bodies, perfect breasts and huge dicks is only going to make any normal boy or girl feel inadequate. However, using your own mind and your own imagination to think of sexy scenes seems like a much more calm and creative way of having a hand gallop.

When fantasies aren't funny

Most of the time, wank fantasies are about thinking of the things you enjoy while giving yourself manual pleasure. Usually they're secret little dreams involving people you know, people you've just met or else they might even be about film stars or celebrities, models, soap stars or singers. And these sorts of mental images can be exciting and satisfying.

Some boys get worried when their fantasies don't fit the way they want to feel. The two sexual fantasies that seem to give boys the most trouble and concern are imagined sexual scenes with either sisters or best friends. These are common fantasies. But what happens is that the person having one gets frightened, because they imagine that these sexual fantasies are bad ones. Fantasizing about sex with your sister or sex with your best friend makes boys think they must be incest-crazed monsters or else potentially gay.

But a fantasy is just a fantasy. It's not reality. As long as you don't act on the fantasy, no one has been harmed and all that's happened is you've had some thoughts that have disturbed you. During your teens, as your sexuality is forming, it's very easy to get confused sexually. A huge number of boys and girls have feelings and fantasies about members of their own sex. Having these thoughts doesn't necessarily mean you are gay or going to be gay. At this stage of your life, feelings of friendship and attraction can often get blurred and confused. Even if you do think you are gay, there's no need to worry. It's still your fantasy and you have every right to it, just as you have every right to express your sexuality with a willing partner.

But if you're having trouble with the fantasies that come into your head, then you can try using pictures for a while or try changing who and what you think about. Or even give up masturbating for a bit. The whole purpose of masturbation is to give yourself pleasure and comfort. If, for whatever reason, it isn't making you happy, then stop. It's not obligatory. You don't have to do it. Some people are happier not wanking.

Wanking with friends

Male There are times when jerking the gherkin is not a solo pursuit. During adolescence, a lot of boys may experiment with tossing off a friend or being tossed off by one. Often at boarding schools or on summer camps boys might get involved in wanking competitions or group-masturbation activity. It's all very normal, if a bit embarrassing.

A lot of guys worry that because they've been experimenting sexually with other boys this means they'll grow up to be gay, or they just worry that they've done something terrible. Be reassured that this sort of stuff goes on all the time. Most of what adolescent sex is about is experimentation and investigation. Boys and girls in single-sex schools don't get the opportunity to experiment with the opposite sex as much as they'd like, so they do the next best thing.

Female The other type of shared masturbation is where you get a hand job from a girlfriend. Having a girl do what you've done a million times yourself gives the whole experience a brand-new and immensely exciting twist. A lot of boys love to have girls tickle their pickle.

But a lot of girls get into a panic because they worry that they won't know how to do it properly or will do something disastrously wrong.

'I'm a fifteen-year-old girl who has a lovely boyfriend. He keeps asking me to "give him a wank" or "toss him off" and I don't know what this means. I would be happy to do it if I knew what it was, but I don't. I can't ask friends or family, it would be too embarrassing.'

Beth

'I would like to know how to wank a boy off. I know it probably sounds silly, but a few nights ago my boyfriend asked me to, and as I'd always read in magazines that it was a very tender area I was extremely gentle. I guess I was too gentle, as he put his hand on mine and applied more pressure. He applied more and more pressure until he eventually came. Now I don't know how much pressure should be applied and how tender the area is.'

Lucy (16)

The Willy in Action

'I was at a party getting off with the boy of my dreams, when he asked me to "toss him off". I was eager but scared I'd do something stupid, so I didn't and still don't really know how to. I quickly changed the subject and we carried on, but all night he kept pushing my hand nearer his penis. I wanted to say yes, but I didn't know what to do.'

James Dean fan (15)

It is completely wrong and offensive for any boy to expect or pressurize a girl into masturbating him. But if both parties are willing, then it makes a lot of sense for a little verbal communication to take place. How is a girl supposed to know what you like? Girls are often more scared of doing something wrong. The whole business about this sort of sexual activity is that it should be done in the most relaxed and exciting way. It's not exciting if you're dead scared of making a fool of yourself. But it *is* exciting to show carefully and share what it is you want, and even to explain what it feels like to be touched that way.

The key to good sex is always good communication. The more you can share your experiences and communicate your desires, the better it will be. Wanking is something you and your girlfriend can enjoy together, not by just doing it but by talking about it too.

LIVING WITH A WILLY

Ejaculation

We can send spacemen to the moon, dig tunnels under the Channel, even design robots that can build anything from Porsches to plasma-screen TVs. But still we can't really compete with the wonders of Mother Nature. In one single ejaculation, in one simple wank's worth of come, there are up to four million sperm. And yet it only takes one sperm to fertilize a female egg. One boy in one week, masturbating twice a day, could produce enough sperm to repopulate the world.

Males tend to forget the wonders of spunk, probably because we see so much of it. It's easily possible to come twice a day 365 days of the year. That means that in sixty years of sex and masturbation you could come nearly 45,000 times. Which, if you average about three and a half million sperm per come, means that in a lifetime you could ejaculate more than 150 billion sperm. This is some serious load.

The average portion of spunk is probably around a teaspoonful in size. Sometimes more, sometimes less. The amount usually relates to how long it is since you last ejaculated. Also, as you get older, you might find that you don't produce so much, so regularly. The peak of your come production is likely to be in your teens and early twenties.

Sometimes your spunk will spurt out of your knob like a rocket launching from Cape Canaveral. It might squirt a metre or so, even whack you in the face while you're having

The Willy in Action

a wank. Other times it might just dribble out the end in one small beady bubble, going nowhere fast.

It can be thick and gloopy, almost pearl-like in colour, or it can be really thin and watery. In all these forms and quantities, it's perfectly normal. And because sperm are microscopic, just a tiny bubble could still be brimming with millions of little soldiers, each of which is enough to get a girl pregnant. It's a point worth noting, that you don't even have to have come to have produced enough sperm to accidentally get someone pregnant. All the more reason to get used to using a condom.

Spunk's got a salty taste and a strong sweetish smell.

Most of the worries that boys have concerning their ejaculations are either about not having started ejaculating at all, which is usually just the consequence of not starting puberty, or else they worry that they come too quickly during sex. And some even worry that they can't come during sex.

But even before sex rears its head, ejaculations can be a problem for other reasons.

'I am a sixteen-year-old boy and the thing is I get erections very easily. Even just looking at a girl's chest makes a bulge in my trousers. That's not a problem, the problem is that when I get an erection I release a lot of sperm. It all seeps through my trousers and mates have even pointed it out and laughed. It sometimes looks like I've wet myself. The worst part is that when it dries it starts to smell.'

Desperate

LIVING WITH A WILLY

Although ejaculation is usually the end product of masturbation or sex, it can also happen just when the penis is aroused and erect. Often some small amount of semen will leak out of the end of your penis when you're getting excited. There's nothing you can do to stop it, it's like a pre-come come.

The important thing to realize though is that this pre-come semen can still contain millions of sperm, so it's just as likely to make a girl pregnant if accidentally transferred to the vagina on fingers.

A leaky dick can be an embarrassment whether it's going to spill some of the seeds early on in the proceedings or leak during your afternoon woodwork lesson. But again, it's no big deal and will probably stop being so active as time wears on. If you do find you tend to cream the inside of your boxers regularly, then obviously it's important to change your underwear at least once a day, use deodorant and even maybe excuse yourself to go to the loo and mop up any excess with toilet paper. Chances are it won't happen that often or for a long period.

Ejaculation usually occurs when you reach a physical sexual climax either through wanking or sex. And it's a very physical event — your heart rate and blood pressure increase, your breathing is often much faster than normal and, as you ejaculate, the muscles in your genital area contract and spunk is pumped out through your penis. It's a big occasion for the body and, because of what goes on, you usually get extremely pleasant sensations, which create an intense moment called an orgasm.

The Willy in Action

Ejaculation is what happens to you physically; it's the act of spurting spunk. But an orgasm is what you *feel*. The two don't always go together. It is possible to have an orgasm and feel all those intense sensations and huge pleasures without ejaculating. And you can ejaculate without having the great feelings. Sometimes when you masturbate it's just a quick squirt with very little feeling at all. Yet sometimes great sex, maybe even sex without penetration, can be so sensual and exciting that you experience orgasmic feelings without ejaculation.

Alcohol doesn't normally help ejaculation or orgasm. Getting drunk can have disastrous short-term effects on your sex life. Too much drink can stop you coming, or can make you come very quickly. It can also affect your erection. 'Brewer's droop', where your dick becomes uncontrollably limp, is a common affliction. The fuzziness of alcohol can spoil an orgasm or inhibit it, or even just make you forget how nice it was. On the whole, booze and sex don't mix well.

A lot of people claim that getting drunk is what gets you sex. It might lower everyone's inhibitions and make them do things they'd think twice about if they were sober, but having sex with some girl who wakes up the next day and really wishes she hadn't slept with you, or else waking up yourself and feeling horribly embarrassed about what you did last night, isn't the best blueprint for a happy healthy sex life.

Drugs, apart from being illegal, do nothing for sex. Heroin can stop you getting a hard-on entirely; speed makes your willy shrink to the size of a petrified whelk;

91

acid is too weird for sex; Ecstasy is often thought to be
the perfect sex drug, but it makes too many people act
stupidly; dope makes you paranoid about everything,
and cocaine, or crack, turns you into a totally
unattractive gibbering monster.

Sex may be a bit scary, it may be a bit difficult
at times, but when it's good, it's heart-stoppingly,
gobsmackingly wonderful. It's such a shame to blur
the ecstatic sensations of sex with a load of low-grade
chemicals. The best sex is pure sex.

Premature ejaculation

Coming too quickly, or the fear of coming too quickly,
has got to rank up high on the all-male Worry Top Ten.
It's like the whole business of big dicks and little dicks;
men have managed to persuade themselves that how
you 'perform' sexually is really important to who you are
and what calibre of man you make.

As usual, this sort of male logic is a load of rubbish. If
you think about it, the concept of premature ejaculation
or coming too quickly suggests that there is a right time
and a wrong time to come. Which isn't strictly true.
Men have decided that the right time to come is after
or at the same time as their female partner comes. The
reasoning behind this is the idea that a 'good lover' or
a 'real man' can hold back his ejaculation until his lover
has enjoyed the sex fully and had her own orgasm.

The Willy in Action

This sort of thinking suggests that all women want, or even are able, to come during penetrative sex (where the penis is inside the vagina), which definitely isn't true. Women are turned on and excited to the extent of orgasm by all sorts of different things, like clitoral stimulation, breast caressing, massage, etc., many of which might not involve the penis at all. So the male coming quickly inside the vagina (or better still, inside a condom inside the vagina) might not even be an issue.

Still, what men have decided is that premature ejaculation, where the male shoots his load 'too soon', is practically a cardinal sin. Yet nearly every male who has had a few sexual encounters will know that sometimes it's impossible not to come quickly, especially early on in your sexual adventures. You can get so worked up and excited that you come at the slightest contact between your todger and your beautiful girlfriend.

Sometimes just a gentle hand laid in your lap can make you pop your cork. It happens. And it has to be said, in many situations, girls can find it immensely exciting that you have come so uncontrollably. When you think about it, it's really quite a compliment. It shows how powerfully attractive she is; how much she absolutely makes you melt with desire. And also, just because you come very quickly the first time, it doesn't mean you won't be able to come again, maybe much slower, after you've given the tackle a little rest.

'My boyfriend was suffering from coming too quickly and he worried that he wasn't satisfying me. But the fact is that we love each other and both know that good sex takes time. All I can say is that I felt flattered I turned my boyfriend on so much. I think that it is awful that boys should feel this way about something that is a natural part of sexual exploration. I think relaxing and not worrying about climaxing is the best way to solve the problem.'

Sue (17)

As usual, girls seem to be a couple of streets ahead of us men in the sensible-thinking department. But despite this, men continue to attach a great amount of shame and inferiority to coming quickly. The stupid thing is that every male knows from masturbating that he doesn't always come in the same duration of time. You can hurry a quick crank before dashing off to school and ejaculate within less than a minute. Or else you could be having a leisurely Sunday afternoon hand shandy with your warmest fantasies, which goes on for a full half-hour.

So it's the same with sex. You might find yourself coming quickly, especially in the early days, but as you get more relaxed, things will slow down. Mostly it's just about getting used to your own body and getting used to intensely exciting sexual situations. Experience and practice give you an ability to control and prejudge the moment of ejaculation, which usually results in being able to stave it off by stopping thrusting and moving for a short while till the feelings pass, or else by simply slowing down the momentum.

The Willy in Action

Men and boys are tough on themselves about the time they take to come.

'I'm nineteen and I have a big problem. I'm going out with a sixteen-year-old girl and we are very serious about each other. But every time we make love I have a premature ejaculation. The longest our lovemaking has lasted is only a few minutes. It makes me feel really depressed and I think my girlfriend doesn't enjoy sex because of this. How can I control my orgasm? It's tearing me apart.'

Matt

'When my girlfriend and I have sex, foreplay lasts quite a long time, then when we start intercourse I ejaculate within a few seconds. We cannot carry on as I lose my erection. We both joke about it, but it makes me feel inadequate.'

Capital Radio fan

'I am a sixteen-year-old boy and I know I have a really bad problem, as my girlfriend gets frustrated. The problem is I don't last very long into sex before I come. A few days ago we spent a day at my house and as soon as I put a condom on and put it inside her I came straight away. Other times on average I last about a minute. I have not spoken to anyone about it because it is so embarrassing. I don't want my relationship to split because I'm not good enough.'

Anon

'I am seventeen and I suffer from premature ejaculation. My problem is that as soon as I become slightly sexually active with a girl, I ejaculate. I'm sure you appreciate the embarrassment and the hampering effects it is having on my sex life. Is there something I can do or take to help me?'

Concerned

There is no right or wrong time to come. Some men come in one minute, others can last fifty minutes. This doesn't mean the man who lasts the longest is the better lover. Sex isn't just about thrusting and pumping away for hours on end. It's about warmth and affection, sensuality and good, friendly, funny communication. A lot of women would agree that just being humped for ages at a stretch is not very sexy or satisfying at all. And the longer the period of time a man can penetrate a woman doesn't mean the greater the chance of her achieving an orgasm. Penetration is not the only key to a woman's pleasure. Many women prefer to be touched and stroked and caressed before and/or during penetration. They find these sensations more exciting and the combination of sensations are what may lead to orgasm.

In saying that, if a man finds he regularly comes more quickly than he and his partner want, then there are things he can do. There are even things they can do together to slow down the orgasm. One technique is to practice masturbating on your own to the point just before you come, then stop. Don't come. Keep doing this for four or five times. And practise this a few times a week. You can even do it with your partner, where she masturbates you until you tell her to stop.

What this does is train you to control your orgasms so that you can recognize the feelings of when you are about to come and can stop in time. It takes practice, but usually it does make a difference.

Sex but no ejaculation

In the same way that many men get upset about coming 'too quickly', loads seem to suffer from exactly the opposite problem where they can't come at all.

'I had sex for the first time with my girlfriend and I really let her down as I didn't reach an orgasm. Is there something wrong with me? My friends all reach a climax. Ever since this we have been drifting apart. I really blame myself, though I have tried to talk to her about it. It may be the end of our relationship, but I still love her. Is it normal for a boy not to reach a climax?'

Anxious (16)

'I am an eighteen-year-old boy. I have been going out with my girlfriend for eight months. We have made love several times. Although my girlfriend is very beautiful and I love her very much, I find that

97

when we are making love, I cannot reach the point of ejaculation. We've found that when we are not making love I can ejaculate by other means. Have I got a major problem inside me? I am also worried that I will never be able to start a family. I feel I am not worthy of her even though she tries to reassure me.'

Worried

Not being able to come during sex is a very common problem. Just like premature ejaculation, it often occurs early on in your sex life, or else at times when sex is a bit stressful. Being with a new girlfriend could make you sexually nervous, which could easily inhibit you and stop you from ejaculating. We should never underestimate how much of the sex goes on inside our heads. We can blame various parts of our body – well, one in particular usually – but the problem is often inside our head. When we get nervous and worked up about sex, the strain shows down below.

Men and boys can get weird about sex. We take so much on board and give ourselves such a hard time about performing well. Then we assassinate ourselves when we think we're 'bad' at sex. We assume that we have failed as men if we've 'failed' at sex. What a lot of tosh!

The less performance-obsessed we can be about sex, the more we can enjoy it and the more real contact and real communication we can have with our partners. If a guy is so intent on lasting twenty-five minutes during penetrative sex, the chances are all his efforts are being concentrated into his dick, keeping it from coming. But if you think about it, this is actually quite off-putting for the woman.

A lot of women complain that a man seems distant and distracted during sex, which is not very flattering or loving for them. This is often because he's concentrating so hard-on not coming, that it's no great turn-on for her. He's just giving himself a hard time and the sex suffers as a result.

It would make much more sense and be much more sexy if there was more communication, more fun and less worry.

Orgasms

To be absolutely blunt, too much fuss is made about orgasms.

Women have historically had a raw deal on the orgasm front. It used to be that a woman's needs and desires weren't considered during sex. Men would just do their bit, have a hump and then come. If the woman got anything out of it, well good for them. But there was never any pressure put on men to help their partners enjoy sex. Traditionally women were meant to 'lie back and think of England'.

Most thoughtful male lovers these days would think

it pointless and unsatisfying to have sex if their partner's feelings and desires weren't taken into consideration. The idea of having sex with a woman and not caring if she's enjoying it is well out of order. You might as well be having sex with a prostitute, where her only interest is the money.

But, in saying that, orgasms are only one aspect of good sex. They're not the be-all and end-all: you don't have to come to have a seriously exciting sexual experience.

Indeed, the quest for the orgasm can get a bit tedious for both men and women. Too much fuss is made about orgasms in books and magazines and films. A lot of people, both men and women, get to feel inadequate about sex if they and their partner aren't coming with great earth-shattering squeals every five minutes. This sort of sex only really exists in the fantasy of Hollywood movies.

Male orgasms are a bit hard to define. Some would say that if you've come, then you've had an orgasm. But that's not strictly true. Sometimes you can ejaculate and feel very little. Other times you can ejaculate, usually during good sex, and it feels like your whole body has been turned inside out.

Orgasms shouldn't be seen as the ultimate goal of sex. If you just view orgasms as the real goal of sex then you can easily end up disappointed. To be too obsessed by orgasms is narrow-minded. There's a lot more to sex than coming.

Orgasms can be a let down. Apart from anything else, when you come, it usually means the end, or the start of

The Willy in Action

the end, of your lovemaking. If you don't come, you can go on doing different things as long as you both enjoy it.

Some people find orgasms a bit scary. The sensations of intense pleasure and of being out of control for a moment can have the effect of making some people feel down and vulnerable.

So much of the stuff written and said about sex deals with the great earth-shattering heights of pleasure that come from orgasm. This is fantasy sex. A lot of times sex is just a comfy, caring, quite pleasurable thing two people who love each other do. It can sometimes be great. It's often just OK. It can be also bad. To get too sensation-seeking about sex will lead to disappointment.

The best thing about sex is not what happens and what you did, it's who you did it with, what you both felt about it and about each other. Sex is not very often a huge, breathtaking ground-breaking event. Most of the time it's just a small, warm comfy-feeling thing.

Feeling iffy without a Stiffy

Next to coming too quickly, the biggest other problem that men have is that they lose their erections before or during sex. Again this is one of those problems that men feel so embarrassed and shameful about that they never discuss it with each other. They're too shy to admit it because they think that their mates will just laugh and take the mickey. The sad thing is that this is probably true.

All the same, problems with erections that won't go up or stay up are very, very common.

'I've started going out with a girl who has a reputation for going out with boys. The problem is I can't get an erection when we start to play with each other. All she can say is, "The other lads got one, why don't you? Don't you love me?" I'm still a virgin at eighteen. Is this a serious problem? I even think of turning gay.'

Joe

'I have been going out with this girl I love for two years. Recently we tried having sex. I brought condoms and was very careful, but my penis wouldn't stiffen up. I am so embarrassed. She was understanding but I knew she was disappointed. Is there something wrong with me?'

Distressed (16)

'I am twenty years old and have been going out with my girlfriend for nearly a year. I'm getting really frustrated because every time we make love I have an erection at first, but when we actually go to do it, the erection goes off. My girlfriend keeps thinking it's because I don't love her. I do. I just can't get it to stay hard.'

Tom

The Willy in Action

'I am seventeen years old. Recently, after discussing it, my girlfriend and I decided to have sex, which was a new experience for both of us. We took all the precautions and once I had an erection I went to put on a condom, but then found I wasn't erect any more. Because of this we couldn't have sex properly. I have tried since but the same thing happened. What is wrong with me? Why can't I put on a condom and stay erect? I feel a failure.'

Anon

'I'm seventeen, and when my girlfriend and I try to make love I can never get an erection even though I'm quite excited. I can get an erection before, but when I put my penis into her I just flop. I have only known my girlfriend for a short while and I think this will put her off me. Even though she seems to be very understanding, she says that it might have something to do with drink. Could this have something to do with it?'

Embarrassed from Leeds

'I have had sexual relationships with girls and I could come with them. With them I would go hard and have an orgasm, but with my new girlfriend I can't even get a hard-on. I am afraid of sex with this girl. I think that if I try to have sex with her I won't come and it would be so embarrassing. I really love her very deeply. This is the best relationship I have ever had with a girl. I am afraid that I will lose her.'

Worried

The willy is an unreliable tool. It's sensitive to stress and often acts in an unpredictable manner. Most men have experienced loss of erection at exactly the moment they would least expect it to happen. Even when they feel very excited and absolutely raring to go, suddenly the willy can shut down all systems and turn back into the warm soft sleepy thing it so often likes to be.

Drink can make it go floppy. So can fitting a condom. Having sex with the most beautiful girl in the world can make it go floppy. Having sex for the first time with a girl, or with someone you really love; or having sex somewhere strange or stressful, expecting your parents to appear home suddenly from the bingo, or doing it in the back of the car. All these things can have a counteractive effect on the todger.

Even nothing in particular or specific can make it go soft. One night, out of the blue, for no apparent reason, your dick could suddenly decide that it's not going to stay hard or even go hard in the first place. Be warned, this does happen and it's perfectly and absolutely, dead-boringly normal.

So you might lose your erection. So what? There's nothing you can do except forget about it, get on with some warm kissing and cuddling, and try again later. Don't try to hide it or get angry or blame your girlfriend.

The Willy in Action

It's far better and far more useful just to have a laugh at the unpredictability of your willy and get on with something else. If you turn it into a big deal you're more likely to upset your partner and yourself and stop yourself from getting hard later.

The more pressure you put yourself under and the more of an issue you turn it into, the more difficult it becomes to function.

Don't ever kid yourself that you're master of the monster inside your Y-fronts. You're not. It'll trip you up (not literally), fool you and fox you, trick you and tease you, embarrass you and abandon you a lot of times, all through your life.

There's nothing you can do about it except accept it. And be assured in the simple knowledge that, even though they never seem to admit it openly, every other male is experiencing exactly the same stuff too, time and time again.

5

Sex and Your Sausage

A priceless organ

There's no doubt about it, the willy is a fabulous organ.
It may not be the most complicated or sophisticated of
our organs, but it certainly delivers a lot more fun than
some of them do. In all my life I can't remember having
one good experience from my liver, or my kidneys come
to that. But the little one-eyed trouser snake has given
me a whole heap of dreamy feelings, heart-stopping
moments and even quite a few laughs.

No matter how brilliant we think our knobs are, there
is no excuse for using them instead of a brain. Too many
males rely on their tackle to make major life decisions,
and this can be a big mistake.

Sex is a very powerful thing. Even after thousands
of years of Man's evolution we are still easily enslaved
to something as basic as sex. You only have to look at
advertising trends to see that we haven't come very far
since our cave-dwelling days!

If a manufacturer wants to sell a new model of motor
car, motorbike, laptop or computer game, what do
they do? They get a bunch of scantily clad models to

stand around it in various states of provocative undress, caressing the aforementioned product, and very quickly men and boys take notice. It doesn't mean we all rush out and empty our savings accounts to buy one. But we sure do tune in to the adverts.

Because sex is so powerful, men and women often make errors of judgement: they find they're too often more influenced by their galloping hormones than by their sense of decency, fair play or conscience.

People start affairs, they have sex before they're ready, they have sex with partners who are obviously the wrong partners, they have sex without contraception or precautions, and then they end up feeling terrible about it afterwards. An awful lot of people have experienced sex that they regret. Lust, alcohol, drugs and, quite often, good old peer pressure have lead countless couples to have the sort of sex they wish they'd never had. It's such a pity. For a moment it might have seemed like a good idea. The moment and the sex soon pass, but the feelings of regret and of letting yourself down can last for a very long time.

First-time sex

It's very hard, especially in your teens when your hormones are tugging you up and down like a yo-yo, to imagine that some sex can be unpleasant or wrong. When your tackle is screaming out to be used, it's easy

Sex and Your Sausage

to think that any sex is good sex. This isn't true. Some sex is awful. Even first-time sex for a lot of people is a major disappointment.

One of the reasons why first-time sex is often so unfulfilling is because people rush into it. Here are a few more:

1. They don't know the person they're having it with well enough.
2. Even if they know them, they haven't thought it through or, better still, talked it through.
3. They aren't relaxed enough or ready enough.
4. They choose to do it somewhere inappropriate or uncomfortable.
5. They don't have enough time to do it justice.
6. They don't really know what they're doing.
7. They haven't got adequate contraception.
8. They've thought too much about just doing it and not enough about what doing it together will mean to their relationship.

It's such a pity to rush into first-time sex, because a lot of boys only end up thinking they're inferior and inadequate, and girls think they've done something wrong. Or didn't do something they should have done.

For boys, being a virgin is often regarded as a 'problem'. Male teenage peer pressure can make it very difficult to be a virgin. Boys often take the mickey out of each other if they haven't had sexual experiences by the age of fifteen or so. They often start publicly ridiculing other boys who haven't started or managed to 'score' in the field of sexual exploration. And so, as a boy you can be forced into making a choice of either lying about your sexual adventures, which many decide is the easiest option, or else you rush into experiences that are inappropriate. Usually with girls you maybe don't know well, don't really like and definitely aren't ready to be intimate with. It's exactly the same for girls.

Being a virgin is made very hard for some boys, not only by other boys, but even by some girls too.

'I am seventeen and still a virgin. My girlfriend keeps pressing me to have sex, but I am too embarrassed because I am not very well developed and don't know much about sex. I am just scared that she will laugh at me and then dump me. Our relationship is very close at the moment and I feel if I don't have sex with her soon it will fail.'

Andy

'I am seventeen-year-old virgin male. I've been seeing a girl of the same age for a fortnight and she was all too keen to have sex. At the crucial moment my nerves got the better of me and I stupidly said, "What do I do next?" My girlfriend finished with me like a shot and I was left the butt of all jokes at college. Apart from the

Sex and Your Sausage

embarrassment of this, my confidence and self-esteem have been shattered. I'm afraid I'll never have the bottle to approach another woman.'

Anon

'I am a fifteen-year-old boy and I have a big problem. You see, all of my friends have lost their virginity and brag about how good it was. I am the only one who has not had sex yet. I really want to impress them. The main problem is that I am ugly and I have no girlfriend. Once or twice I have considered prostitution, but I know this is a dirty thing to do. How can I get the girls to like and have sex with me before my friends find out I'm a virgin?'

Anxious

In some boys' minds, sex becomes this sort of abstract thing that's not connected to relationships or love. It's just something you have to do in order to earn your place among your peer group. Apart from anything else, this suggests that the quality of sex, and the quality of any emotion that goes on between the two people having sex, is not as important as the impressed reaction of your mates. If boys are only having sex to impress their mates, then is it any wonder so many girls feel they get a raw deal?

A lot of girls have sex with the wrong boy or have sex before they feel ready and soon wish they hadn't.

LIVING WITH A WILLY

'I feel cheap and nasty because of something that recently happened to me. We went clubbing, and after a drink I ended up gong back to this lad's house with my friend. I ended up having sex with this guy, who I had never met before. I wanted to wait until I'd found the right person as I was a virgin. I feel I have betrayed myself.'

Distressed (17)

'I was going out with this boy for just over a month. He was really popular at school and it was a dream come true that he was actually mine. Almost all my friends were speaking of their experiences and I had nothing to say. I felt I was being left behind. I knew he wouldn't say no, because he was quite experienced, so I made a move and we ended up having sex. My first time was not one to remember. For the first few days I was glad I had something to say when the topic was brought up, but soon I began to regret it. We broke up not long after. I discovered having sex doesn't mean you're grown up.'

Lucy (15)

One of the cruel ironies of life and society is that boys think they are more attractive and acceptable to girls if they have lost their virginity. Yet some girls are made to feel ashamed if they have had too many sexual experiences.

Sex and Your Sausage

'I am eighteen and have had two sexual
relationships. One with a boy I was going with
for eighteen months, and the other with someone
I used to see from time to time. Now I have met
someone who I think is a virgin. I like him a lot,
but my problem is that I'm racked with guilt.
I'm too scared of getting involved in another
relationship because, aside from possibly making
another mistake, I'll have to explain my past. If a
girl explained this to you, would you think her a
slag?'

Deborah

There's a misplaced belief among some males that being
a bit of a lad and having sown your wild oats makes
you a thoroughly lived-in man of the world.

Strangely enough, most women don't actually see the
practice of bonking-anything-with-a-pulse as an attractive
element of a man's character. But a lot of boys think this
is what you're supposed to do. They get dragged into
another one of those male-generated myths about being
a stud. Lads think they'll appear more impressive to their
mates if they're seen to be putting it about. The trouble
is, they worry too much about their mates' reactions and
don't even consider any females' point of view.

Some boys seriously think that by having had a
variety of sexual experiences it will make them
attractive to girls. They firmly believe that being a
virgin means no girl will want to go out with them and

they definitely won't have sex with them.

A lot of girls who've written to me say exactly the opposite. Not only are girls not put off by boys being virgins, they actively prefer virgin boyfriends.

'I would definitely prefer to lose my virginity to a boy who was also a virgin. Even if I was experienced, I'd be perfectly happy to have sex with a boy who was still a virgin. I consider them a great turn-on!'

Vicky (15)

'I think being a virgin is a really attractive quality in a boy. I hate boys who go around bragging how many girls they've slept with. They are a real turn-off. Being a virgin shows that he is a caring and mature guy who hasn't just slept with every girl he's been out with.'

Reeta (17)

'I would love to go to bed with a virgin. I lost my virginity when I was fourteen. The guy I lost it to wasn't a virgin and I felt very uncomfortable. It was a total non-event and I thought I hadn't done something right. We hate each other now and I wish I was a virgin so I could lose my virginity to someone who loved me and was also a virgin.'

Kelly (16)

Sex and Your Sausage

'I find it a real turn-off if a boy's had sex before, because I feel intimidated by his experience. If ever I went to bed with a male who wasn't a virgin I'd be embarrassed, because he'd expect me to know what to do as well.'

Anon (14)

So a lot of boys lie about their experiences, or else suffer sexual experiences that they don't enjoy, in order to brag to their mates and raise their status as non-virgins. But the truth of the matter is, that if they could just admit to being inexperienced and virgins, then a whole lot of girls would probably find them more attractive and easier to go out with in the first place. Duh!

In fact these days quite a few teenagers, both male and female, are actively proud of their virginity. Some even wear purity rings to show that they are waiting to get married to a 'special someone' before they have sex. OK, so you may not want to take things that far, but waiting for someone special to have sex with can really be worth it. And, what's more, many girls would definitely appreciate it.

While the idea of a purity ring and a wait-until-we're-married pact might all sound a little cultish and freaky, the notion behind it is perfectly sound. It's simply about looking after yourself, and looking out for yourself. It's about saving your virginity, cherishing it even, until you know the time and the partner are absolutely right for you – rather than just squandering it on a messy bout of fumbly sex that ends up making you squirm a bit, with regret.

It all comes back to that business of not having sex for the sake of impressing others. Not being more concerned about what your mates think of you than the quality of the sex and the emotion involved. Or indeed what your sex partner feels about the whole deal.

Having sex for the sake of sex is often a very empty and unfulfilling experience, but having sex simply for the sake of bigging-up your reputation among your mates is just very, very sad.

Sex without the Sausage

When you think about it, the idea of virginity and sexual 'experience' is a very weird business. Technically speaking you are no longer a virgin when you have finally played hide the sausage with a girl. As soon as your penis has entered a girl's vagina, you are no longer a virgin.

But what's the big deal? The act of slipping a penis inside a vagina is not in itself any great wonderful achievement, especially as the chances are you'll come within seconds and the whole thing will be over before it's really started.

All the same, as soon as the thing's in there, technically you're no longer a virgin. It's daft. To think that the very basic, minimal and often deeply unsatisfying event of this first entry can carry such

Sex and Your Sausage

weighty significance in the eyes of boys is laughable.

Most boys would actually become much better lovers and much more sensual men if they forgot about their dicks for a while in relation to sex. An eagerness to plunge it into a vagina means that the whole event will soon be over, which really does miss the point and also misses so much other good stuff along the way, by being too focused on the penetration.

Sex that doesn't involve penetration can include stuff like mutual masturbation, where you both caress and stimulate each other's genitals by hand. Then there's oral sex, where you excite each other by licking or sucking each other's nipples and sex organs.

Then there's great stuff that doesn't involve the sex organs at all. Stuff like massaging each other's bodies, rubbing oil all over each other, from top to toe, in a warm candlelit room. Or playing striptease, watching each other slowly, slowly undressing and drinking in every tantalizing bit of newly exposed flesh.

All these sensual, sexy things take a little bit of imagination and effort, but they pay off big dividends in the long run. They can spice up and prolong your sex or they can be an alternative to always playing hide the sausage and aiming for penetration. There is so much more to sex than simply using the thing that hangs between your legs.

LIVING WITH A WILLY
Deep frenchy Snogging

French kissing is one of the mysterious wonders of the world. We all grow up thinking it's some sort of really exotic, complicated and deeply naughty kissing ritual that is about as close to sex as you can get without actually having it.

This, of course, is a load of rubbish. French kissing is simply about kissing with your mouth open wide enough to slide your wet pink tongue into the mouth of the person you're kissing. Or else to allow their tongue into yours.

People get hung up about French kissing. They think that it's so complicated that they won't be able to do it right and the world and their whippet will laugh at them for evermore. The thing is, French kissing is easy if you don't try too hard. If you thrust your tongue into someone's mouth and swirl it around like a demented cement mixer, it's not very pleasant for anyone concerned.

The best French kisses start very slow and tentatively with your tongues just hardly touching but gradually getting slightly deeper into each other's mouths, but only if both parties are keen. The worst thing in the world is being really deeply kissed when that's not what you want.

Some people don't like French kissing. It's not everyone's cup of tea by a long shot. A good kisser is not someone who can swish around with his tongue for hours on end. A good kisser is someone who can listen to and feel what the person he's kissing likes. He's also someone who can talk to the person he's kissing before and after those kisses, making them all the more intimate and personal.

Good kissing's not about technique – it's about the feeling. You can be kissed by the world's most practised kisser, but if you've got no feelings for them, it won't be half as good as a tiny peck from someone you adore.

Bragging

There are two main types of bragging. There's bragging about the size of your knob and bragging about what you've done with it.

Some boys love to give their todgers pet names. Stuff like Harry, Hercules, Big Boy, the Beast, Lollypop, Rocky and Giant Jake are pretty much par for the course.

I used to work in a pub with a guy who was always talking about his dick. It was really quite off-putting. He'd even talk about how big it was and what he liked to do with it and the things girls said when they saw it. I could never quite work out why he was telling me. Was it to impress me? To make me feel inferior? I really don't know. He talked about it as though it was a person; sometimes called it his 'Little Brother' or his 'Old Man'.

The other common brag is when boys tell you in every intimate detail what they did with what girl, where and when. Again the suggestion is that you're supposed to be impressed, in awe of them and jealous that they have such good luck with the opposite sex.

But you can't help thinking, if they're having such a good time with all this, why do they have to tell me? It's as though they have to brag about it to make it seem good.

I know myself, I've been guilty of bragging about sex when I was younger, and I know I didn't tell the truth. Not only did I exaggerate some of the details; also I made it out to be something really great, when in truth there were times I didn't think it was that great. But by lying, I could almost persuade myself it was good and that it was worth doing.

Bragging can be just an elaborate way of lying to yourself about the disappointment you feel. If you can legitimize something by telling all your mates what a great time you had, then you don't have to feel bad about it. Yet we boys do this a lot of the time; we're not honest about how things really feel or really affect us. Instead we lie, not just to others but to ourselves. By lying we never have to face our real feelings, which means we never change the way we are. Which is a pity, because then we just go on making the same mistakes and feeling worse and worse about it inside.

By putting on a brave face, we only cover up the truth. And the other damaging thing is that by lying to mates we encourage others to go off and do the same thing. And the lie continues. If they feel bad about it or don't have a good time, they think that there's something wrong with them. But instead of admitting their fears,

Sex and Your Sausage

they lie. And so it goes on.

Bragging about sex, especially sex that was disappointing, is the start of a lie that can continue through a lifetime. And the sad part is that if you could admit there's maybe something wrong or something you're not sure about, there's a good chance you could get to the root of the problem and solve it. But if you just lie to cover it up, then you might be stuck with it for life.

Condoms

Considering that condoms were specifically designed for men to wear during sexual intercourse, we don't have a very good track record of using them. Sure, as lads we've always been very good at taking them into the toilets, turning them into water bombs and chasing Year 7s around the playground with them. But using them for the purpose for which they were intended is another matter.

There are a lot of stupid male myths that make condoms seem uncool. Men claim that they ruin sex; that sex in condoms feels like 'taking a bath in your wellies' or 'eating a Mars bar with the wrapper on'. Some men claim that sex with condoms isn't as good as 'real sex'. Or even that sex with condoms is for kids and beginners, that real men don't use them. As usual this is all tripe of the first order.

121

LIVING WITH A WILLY

The fact of the matter is that these days, with all the elaborate sexually transmitted diseases that are on offer, including HIV, it makes sense to wear a condom. And by wearing a condom you're not only showing sense and respect to your own todger, you're also showing that you care about the health of your partner. Condoms, and other forms of contraception such as the Pill, are also a must when it comes to avoiding pregnancy, which is a pretty big issue when you're having sex with someone. Never just assume that a girl is on the Pill – and, even if she is, you should still use a condom, for health reasons. Wearing a condom is a sign of respect. It shows you respect yourself and you respect your partner. It also helps both of you relax. By wearing a condom, it means you can enjoy sex without having nagging worries and concerns, causing tension between you, when you both want to be free to relax and get immersed in the intimacy of each other's bodies.

Of course there are some guys who think that taking the risk of catching a disease or getting a girl pregnant all adds to the excitement of the sex. This is a bit like saying that driving a car with dodgy or no brakes makes your motoring more fulfilling.

Of course there may be times when using a condom does make you lose your erection. The business of faffing around getting it out of the packet might take the edge off your stiffy. But as we all know, stiffies are not all that hard to come by. With a little care and attention from you or your partner, your knob can soon be back to peak firmness.

Sex and your Sausage

And the opposite can also be said for condoms — they can sometimes improve and enhance your sex. For a start there's all that business of getting your partner to put the condom on for you. Many is the game that can be played out while putting on a johnny. Apart from anything else, it means that you'll get your willy touched and caressed in the process.

It's also a very good way for your partner to get to know your willy. Many girls never really get to touch and investigate a knob, because its owner is too shy to show it, or just far too eager to plunge ahead. As we all know, willies may not be the prettiest creation in the universe, but they are damned interesting things to fiddle about with. Especially if you haven't got one of your own. It seems unfair to deprive your partner of the pleasure.

And the whole business of putting on a condom means that you have to stop or at least slow down the progress of your sexual adventure. This can often provide a very useful little rest moment. If you don't stop, and instead you just plough straight on, getting more and more excited with what you're doing, chances are you'll get too excited and come before you or your partner have had that much of a chance to enjoy the penetration.

But by stopping to put a condom you may well find that you can actually gain better control of your orgasm. Taking a break to put on a condom and even the wearing of a condom can definitely help delay you coming so quickly.

LIVING WITH A WILLY

It doesn't help that condoms are thought to be a bit tricky and technical to use (see page 130). There are a lot of different types of condom and they each come with instructions. All the same, some boys do get scared about not knowing what to do with them. It's that same old problem again: boys don't know something, but feel they ought to know, so they become too embarrassed to ask anyone because then they'll look a fool. So instead they pretend they do know. Or else they go to elaborate lengths to avoid drawing attention to the things that they don't know.

Basically, we are very scared of looking stupid or inexperienced, so we avoid doing things that are going to catch us out. A condom may be one of those things.

'I am going out with a sixteen-year-old girl. I like her very much and don't want to lose her. She says she wants to go to bed with me. I wasn't sure, so I suggested we wait. But I think she will finish with me if I don't make a move soon. I don't want to lose her, because she's the best thing that's ever happened to me. But I have a problem: I don't know how to use a condom.'

Anxious

The range and variety of condoms on sale can seem like a minefield from the start. There are all these different brands and styles, but sometimes having too much choice can just be baffling. If we

Sex and your Sausage

don't actually know what the difference between various condoms is, or which ones will do what to us, or to our partner, then we sink into dazed-and-confused mode. Again, we're scared we'll do or choose something wrong or naff and end up looking like a right plonker.

'Me and my girlfriend both feel we are ready to have sex. But I want to know which condoms are the best. I want to use Durex, but there are at least five types. What are the differences and which would protect me and my girlfriend best?'

David

'I'm worried. I love my girlfriend very much and I am wondering which condoms are the most protective and reliable ones. I want this to be very special for my girlfriend.'

Leigh

'I've been going out with this girl for three years. We have decided to have sex. Can you tell me which condoms are the most protective and how to go about having sex with her? I really want it to be special.'

Worried

'My girlfriend and I are thinking of having sex for the first time and want to take precautions, but we are not sure what to use. What types of condoms are there; are there different sizes; which are the most reliable and safest condoms, and which are the best makes?'

Dale

Since HIV, condoms have become more and more important – not just as a means of contraception, but also as protection. Although they aren't totally safe, using condoms makes sexual intercourse much safer and greatly reduces the risk of catching or transmitting any infections.

Their new-found importance has meant that condom manufacturers and marketing people have gone over the top trying to persuade the public to buy their products. They've done this by making them more exotic and unusual, with different sorts of ribbing and raised bumps, and even by making them in a variety of colours and flavours. This might make them more attractive on one level, but it also makes them more confusing to buy. When there were just a couple of brands available, then you couldn't really go far wrong.

These days, there are basically six different types of condom you can buy:

Avanti Ultima is a Durex condom that is made for anyone who knows they are allergic, or thinks they might be allergic, to latex, which is the material condoms are normally made from. These are made of another 'revolutionary' material, and most people who suffer allergic reactions to condoms find these non-latex ones work a treat.

Sex and your Sausage

Flavoured: there are hundreds of different exotic flavours of condom, from chocolate mint to pina colada. Durex do a select-flavours pack which includes orange, banana, strawberry and even kiwi-flavoured condoms. The idea of the flavouring is simply to make them more fun and more tasty during oral sex.

Ribbed: brands like Durex Pleasuremax or Sensation and Mates Intensity have rings of raised rubber ribs or rubber studs or raised dots along their length in order to give extra sensation inside the girl's vagina during sex.

To add to the range of condoms that offer extra sensations, there are ones that are coated with a special lubricant which creates a tingling sensation for both man and woman when used. The Durex version is called simply Tingle. They also make a warming one called Pleasuremax Warming, which is coated with a warming lube to provide a little extra sensation of heat in the bedroom.

Extra strong: Mates Super Strong or Durex Extra Safe are made thicker than other condoms for extra safety. These are often used by gay men who want to enjoy safe anal sex.

Extra thin: brands like Durex Fetherlite, Durex Elite and Mates Ultra Thin are made thinner for extra sensitivity.

Extra big: there are a couple of brands like Kimono

LIVING WITH A WILLY

Maxx and Trojan Magnum and Durex Comfort XL that are designed especially for boys who have big ego problems and think they need bigger condoms. Who knows? Maybe they really do.

One important rule to stick to when you're buying condoms is that you check that they've got the British Standards Kitemark printed on the packet. What this means is that they've been through rigorous safety checks. If you buy ones that don't have the Kitemark, you don't know how dependable they're going to be.

Anyone who's ever been fishing probably knows the saying that 'most fishing tackle is designed to catch the fisherman, not the fish'. It's the same with condoms. You can fall into the trap of thinking that a coconut-flavoured, extra-ribbed pink one with a tickling tip is going to make you the dog's bollocks when it comes to hot loving. Not true. A fancy condom does not a good lover make. Most of the time, it's best to keep things simple and concentrate on being kind, warm, loving and understanding.

'My boyfriend won't wear condoms. He refuses to wear them because he says they are embarrassing. How can I get him to wear a condom to get over his embarrassment?'

Dominique

'I am a troubled eighteen-year-old. I want to have sex with my boyfriend. He's the first boy I've ever been serious about and I'm afraid of losing him.

Sex and your Sausage

I don't want to go on the Pill as it's bad for my health, but my boyfriend refuses to wear condoms. He says that they're embarrassing to buy. What can I do to change this?

Sarah

Buying condoms can be a bit embarrassing, because no matter what the person who is serving you really thinks, you can always imagine they're having a laugh or a scowl at what you might be about to do with these condoms. Buying them from teenage shop assistants can be hard. There's no doubt about it – there's something very disquieting about buying condoms from someone you'd actually quite fancy using them with.

That's why vending machines in gents' toilets were invented. In pubs and clubs and some train stations you can serve yourself in the privacy of a public lavatory. In supermarkets you can get them and bury them in among a load of non-embarrassing gear. In petrol stations you can buy them off glassy-eyed cashiers who couldn't give a monkey's if you were the Pope. Or you can buy them online and no one will be any the wiser. Durex now has a very stylish and accessible website with plenty of facility to buy online, and there're also tons of individual online pharmacies and sex shops where you can buy every brand of condom know to Man.

LIVING WITH A WILLY

Practice!

There is no point going to all the trouble of buying condoms and carrying them around for weeks, months and years, if, when it comes to the big moment, you can't get one to go on right. And let's face it, when you are about to have sex, maybe for the first time, chances are you'll be nervous, your hands will be shaking, your heart pounding and your mind will be on something much more engaging than what it says on the instructions inside the pack.

So the answer is, don't wait until the big moment before you fit a condom for the first time!

Practise at home. Take a few condoms into your bedroom and experiment with them. Try fitting one. Have a wank with one on. Try putting them on in the dark. Try fitting them with one hand. Try everything. The better you know your way around a condom, the more time you get to concentrate on and enjoy the sex you're about to have.

Remember, forewarned is forearmed and all that guff.

Getting round to using them

Even if you're one of those sensible lads who doesn't believe all the myth and tosh about condoms being bad news, it still doesn't mean you'll know how to use one. Every packet has a little sheet of instructions that it

Sex and your Sausage

would be wise to read and follow carefully.

First make sure that the condom is the right way round. There's often a little teat at the top for catching the spunk. Make sure this is sticking out. Squeeze it between your thumb and forefinger to make sure the air is expelled. This is really important, as if there is air left inside, it can cause the condom to burst or split during sex. Fit it over the tip of your penis, then, while still squeezing the teat, unroll the condom down the length of your penis, right to the base. If the condom is on inside out, you won't be able to unroll it all the way. It's very easy to accidentally put one on inside out. It's by far the most common mistake. If you have got it inside out, don't try to unroll it or flip it around. Try again with a new condom, remembering to squeeze the teat to expel any air.

After you've come, hold the condom in place round the base of your penis as you carefully withdraw from the vagina. This stops it slipping off or any spunk escaping down the side of the condom.

Condoms slipping off seems to be quite a common worry.

'I use condoms with my girlfriend because I think they're the best contraception you can get and I don't want to get her pregnant. I've tried all different types of condoms, but they keep falling off. I am a bit small. Could this be the problem?'

Don

131

LIVING WITH A WILLY

'My problem is that all the girls that I've had serious relationships with have finished with me because my Durex keeps slipping off during intercourse. I can't understand why this happens, because I follow all the directions on how to put them on. My last relationship fell apart because of this problem. What can I do to improve my love life?'

Colin

Condoms don't just slip off of their own accord. Usually what happens is that your erection might dwindle a bit during sex, making them come loose. The trick is to keep checking that it's in place while you're making love, in case it slips, and always make sure you withdraw just after you've come.

If a condom does slip off, or if by any chance it splits during sex, don't keep quiet and pretend it hasn't happened. Be honest and own up, because the risk is that your girl could get pregnant. If a condom has fallen off or split, she will be able to go to the doctor or a Family Planning Clinic to get a morning-after pill. This can be taken up to seventy-two hours after sex. This pill acts as a post-sex contraceptive and will stop her becoming pregnant. Using it is pretty unpleasant for your girl to go through – so don't ever regard this as an easy alternative to proper condom use. It's a contraceptive to be used only in an emergency.

Sex and Your Sausage

Talking about condoms

Some men are scared of condoms, some are flummoxed by them and some aren't quite sure which ones to use. But nearly every bloke is shy of talking about condoms. Then again, so are many girls.

The thing is, you feel you can't get on to the subject if it's early in the relationship. Like you've just sat down for your first burger together and you launch into, 'Which do you prefer, ribbed or flavoured?' It wouldn't work, would it? For a start it's presumptuous – you don't want to jump the gun and talk about sex when you're still nowhere near finding out if it's even on the cards or not.

Also, a lot of blokes don't want to take any responsibility for contraception. They'll use contraception if they're asked to and if a condom is provided, but they believe it's ultimately the girl's responsibility. If she wants to use one, then she has to come up with the goods.

Not all men are like this. As we've seen from the letters, a lot of them are very concerned about keeping sex special and safe. That still doesn't mean they're quite ready to talk about condoms, sometimes they need encouragement. It might also help to know that girls have exactly the same worries.

'I don't want to catch AIDS or get pregnant, but I don't want to go on the Pill, so condoms seem the only way out. I haven't asked my boyfriend about condoms. I haven't had the chance. It's not the type of thing that you'll talk about over the phone with your mum listening in. I really love him and want to have sex with him. I don't know how to bring up the subject of condoms. Do you have any ideas?'

Sally

Talking about condoms isn't going to be easy. It's daft to pretend that there's any simple formula for getting into a sensible chat about condoms with your partner. The thing is not to leave it too late. Don't wait until you're both hot and excited in bed and there're no condoms within ten miles, because then you might just do it without one and live to regret it.

If you think you might possibly, maybe have sex, then make sure some are handy. Don't try and talk about them in some really difficult situation that might be embarrassing, like on the bus or in front of her whole family at Sunday lunch.

There's no point in pretending that condoms fall naturally into conversations – they don't. They need to be introduced. Obviously the worry is that if you introduce them too early you might be seriously jumping the gun, making wild assumptions about what the next stage in your relationship might be, and so scare off the very person you're trying to get closer to.

But by talking about condoms before you get to the point of no return, you are showing a great respect for your partner and a real level of responsibility.

Sex and Your Sausage

For boys who want to use condoms it's easy — they can simply put one on. For girls it's more difficult — they have to persuade the boy to wear one. The earlier this is tackled, the better.

Look upon being able to talk about sex and condoms as a good indication of how well you know each other and how comfortable you are together. If you can't talk about sex or mention condoms, then the chances are you aren't really ready to be having sex together anyway.

Oral sex

In my problem-page postbags, oral sex is big news. You can guarantee every week there'll be a collection of letters on the subject. And nearly every single one of those is from a girl. Most of the time the letters want to know what a blow job is and how to give one.

A blow job is simply when a willy gets sucked, licked and kissed. In the process of all this oral attention, the owner of the willy might experience an orgasm and come, or else he might just get to feel all manner of delicious sensations. Or he might not even like it.

There's no doubt blow jobs can be a lot of fun. Having your dick sucked can be a most enjoyable and erotic experience. But it's not the be-all and end-all of life itself.

The thing is, blow jobs are bit weird, a bit different

and a bit sexually sophisticated. They require a bit more devotion and effort on the part of the giver than say a quick handjob does, and they have a certain different feel to penetrative sex. There's no getting away from it, the sensations of having a soft warm mouth wrapped around your willy can be very nice. Although teeth and dental braces can sometimes be an uncomfortable extra.

Nice or not, let's not turn this simple physical sexual act into some sort of religion. Part of the pleasure of being given oral sex is the comfort of knowledge that the person doing it wants to be doing it. Much as we may love and cherish our todgers, the thought of putting it in our own mouths is probably not something we'd go a real bundle on. So partly it's the surprise and excitement that a girl should be at all willing to do something as intimate as this that has a sensational effect.

Blow jobs are different from sex as well because they are a passive act. You just have to lie or stand while it's done to you, rather than it being something you're doing to, or with, your partner.

It has to be said that blow jobs are not always that effective. Many males find it a lot harder to come from being sucked than they do from being tossed off or having sex, because the actual physical pressure just isn't of the same intensity. Blow jobs are often better when used as part of the overall foreplay to sex, rather than having to star as the main event. In fact, too much concentration on the blow job itself and not enough attention to the overall business of being sexually intimate can lead to a lost erection and a very stiff jaw.

Sex and Your Sausage

Blow jobs all too often become a sort of sex myth with boys, and also with girls. Like they are so special and so naughty and so grown up that every girl should know how to give one and every boy should have had one. The worst thing about blow job is that they've become this big-deal part of teenage sex. So many boys seem to have got it into their heads that they haven't really lived until they've had their willy in some girl's mouth. And, as a result, some boys put pressure on girls to give them blow jobs. And girls feel inadequate if they don't want to do it, or don't feel confident about how to do it.

What could be worse than sucking someone's penis when you don't really want to do it, or aren't even sure what it is you're exactly meant to be doing? It's all part of that rather sick, point-scoring aspect of sex, which requires we perform in some certain way. A blow job is definitely something that should never be forced or pressured.

In saying that, most of the letters I get are from girls who do want to give blow jobs but don't know how.

'I've been going out with this lad for quite a while now and I'm really in love with him. I would do anything for him. The other day he asked me to give him a blow job. I told him maybe the next time, but the problem is I don't really know what it means.'

Karen (16)

'We are two fifteen-year-old girls who have older boyfriends. The problem is that we would like to go further than kissing, but we don't know much about sex. The two of us would like to know what a blow job is and how to do it, because we don't want to feel like silly little girls.'

Louise and Karen

'I am seventeen and my boyfriend is eighteen. He recently asked me to give him a blow job. I have made excuses as to why I don't give him them, but the real reason is that I don't know how to. I don't know how long I can come up with different excuses. My boyfriend is beginning to think that I don't love him. But I do very much and I want to make him happy.'

Depressed

In nearly all the letters I get, the idea of having oral sex has been raised by boys. Girls do seem to want to comply and show willing, but they aren't the ones that started the ball rolling in the first place. Not surprisingly, I've had very few letters from boys whose girlfriends want the boys to give them oral sex. There's definitely something about being given oral sex that appeals strongly to the male but doesn't seem to be being reciprocated in favour of girls.

Giving a boy a blow job shouldn't be seen as some sort of test of love and devotion. Some boys seem to emotionally blackmail girls into giving them oral sex as a way of proving their love. This is all wrong. Any sort of sex that has to be forced or contrived is bad.

No one should feel obliged or pressured into having any sort of sex before they decide they want to. That's not what sex is about. Sex is about progressing and developing at your own natural pace and doing things because you and the person you're doing them with enjoy it. Not because everyone else in your year claims they've done that thing already.

And blow jobs are not by any means an essential part of sex. A lot of girls don't like giving them and many boys don't feel comfortable about being given them. Some guys find it very hard to come. Some feel dead embarrassed having their lover's head bobbing around between their knees. And let's face it, conversation and sweet talking are a vital part of lovemaking. The more you talk and tease each other, the more intimate your lovemaking will seem. But if one of you has permanently got their mouth full, the conversation can get very one-sided.

Just because blow jobs sound exotic and a bit naughty doesn't mean they're crucial.

I think there's a risk that blow jobs become too much the main currency of teenage sex. It's like, boys want to experience a blow job, so they pressurize girls into giving them. And so girls then just see blow jobs as another 'hurdle' of their teens that they need to cross, a bit like losing their virginity. Girls can get very competitive with each other about sexual experiences and egg each other on, or brag to each other, in the same way as boys do.

LIVING with a WILLY

Tragically, many girls end up losing their virginity or giving some boy a blow job, not because they particularly want to, but because they want to impress, or simply keep up with, their mates.

If blow jobs happen naturally as part of the sexual exploration and enjoyment that you have with your partner, then they can be a whole heap of fun. But if they have to be forced, or make you or your partner feel guilty or uncomfortable, they are not worth having.

6

Any Other Business

Testicles

If you thought your knob was a weird-looking thing
– what about your balls?! Maybe I'm biased, but I've
always thought that women's bodies are things of great
beauty. Even their sex organs are visually stimulating.
Breasts are gorgeous, rounded sensual delights. And the
sight of a smooth stomach arcing down to a triangle
of fine pubic hair is a groin-stirring vision. But a pair of
knackers? I don't think so.

They're a strange invention. They're housed in your
scrotal sac which has a different-coloured skin from the
rest of your body. A reddish pink if you've got white
skin and a dark purple if you've got black. The skin tone
actually changes during puberty as your testicles start
to get bigger. The skin that surrounds them gets baggier
and more wrinkly and usually each of your bollocks
hangs at a different height.

In most adult men the left testicle is lower than the
right one. The reason for this is so that when you're
running they don't crush together; one can comfortably
sit just above the other.

LIVING with A WILLY

The scrotum (which is the 'sac' of skin which holds the testicles beneath the penis) is where the sperm are made and stored ready for ejaculation. Sperm are very iffy about temperature, and actually like the climate to be a little lower than body temperature. That's why the balls dangle down away from the body, to keep them cool. And that's why wearing tight, constricting underwear is not good for your fertility: basically you're overheating your sperm.

It's the same in reverse, when you climb out of a freezing swimming pool and your knackers are bunched up like two walnuts in a prune skin. They do that because they're trying to keep up as close to your body as they can, to grab a little heat.

Bollocks seem badly designed. There you are, carrying the future of your race, all your stored-up seed, in a puny little sac dangled daftly between your legs. Meanwhile your brain – a clever organ, though not quite clever enough to reproduce itself – is housed in a case of bone tougher than concrete!

Because of the precarious positioning of the testes, it's important to take care of them while doing dangerous things like hockey, cricket, boxing or karate. A box or cup protector should be worn at all times of sporting danger, to keep things sweet.

Losing a testicle is not the end of the world. Men who've lost one either through accident or disease can normally still have children. It seems we got given a pair just in case we lost one.

Any Other Business

Will you look at those bollocks!

One of the things most schoolboys do at some time or other is kick each other in the nuts. It's hard to say exactly why, it's just another one of those bizarre male rituals we get so attached to. There's hardly a Year-8 lad in the land who hasn't felt the boot or knee of some overactive, hormonally fuelled Year 10 boy in his delicate knackers.

And does it hurt? Does a bear poop in the woods! There is no awful feeling like it in the whole world. The front of your face goes fuzzy, your balls go numb and then this dark evil ache starts in the very pit of your privates and oozes out like lava over your whole body, engulfing you in a sick-making, throat-bulging nausea.

In my school, older boys used to think it was a great sport to walk up to a lad a couple of years younger and shout 'Cough!' at the same time. Needless to say, I did my fair share of writhing around the playground yowling like a cat with its tail in a shredder, while cradling and comforting my aching goolies.

It's not surprising then that we aren't in a great hurry to carry out testicular self-examinations later in life. Most of the sensations associated with testicles are uncomfortable ones. Balls are round sensitive objects that shrivel up and die in the cold or else dangle and flop in the warm. Apart from their weather-related texture changes we don't generally take a whole lot of notice of them.

LIVING with a WILLY

But on the subject of doctors and health, bollocks are important. Testicular cancer is one of the more common forms of cancer to affect young men: nearly a thousand new cases are diagnosed every year. It's a cancer of the sperm-forming cells, and young men are most vulnerable to it because it gets a grip when the hormones are working flat out producing sperm.

The good news is that it's a comparatively easy cancer to treat and can be cured. The thing is to detect it early. This is why we have to overcome any testicle trepidations and have a good old gander at those bollocks on a regular basis.

Genital health, or learning to look after your tackle, must always include an easy and regular relationship with your doctor, but it also requires a certain amount of vigilance on your own part. It's a bit like taking a peek under the bonnet of your car before you go on a long journey, to check you've got enough oil and no unpleasant knocking noises. So the same is required to happily maintain your string and nugget set.

The first sign of trouble in testicles is usually a swelling in one ball and maybe a dull ache in the lower stomach or in the bollock itself. In order to keep aware of what's going on down below, it's important to have a proper peek yourself.

Just after you've had a hot bath, stand in front of a mirror and cup your cods in the palm of your hand. One ball is often a bit larger than the other, which is perfectly normal. What isn't normal are any lumps or bumps on the curving front or underside surface of the testicle.

Any Other Business

There is a thing at the top and the back of the bollock called the epididymis, which is a sort of squiggly lumpy structure where the sperm are stored and ripen. This is meant to be there. But any pea-shaped lumps you can feel sticking up on the rest of the ball are not meant to be there. If there's anything strange and out of place, then don't panic, just go and tell your doctor.

Doing a testicular examination once a month is an easy and sensible way to look after your tackle and keep ahead of any possible problems.

Foreskin hygiene is very important as well. Washing properly under and around your foreskin twice a day can ward off bacterial infection and possibly even help guard against penile cancer. Keep it clean and tidy, and not only is it going to be nicer to use and more pleasant for anyone else to handle, it'll also last a lot longer too.

Although a lot of males get totally obsessed by the size and shape of their tackle, there are an awful lot who don't do anything to look after it. Rather than just regarding it as something useful to pee through, fun to play with and ever ready for the occasional spot of love-action, it makes much more sense to treat it as a constant companion.

Just like a car, instead of always having a job for it to do every time you take it out of the garage, it's nice, once in a while, to wheel it out purely for a bit of tender loving care and attention.

We expect a lot from our three-piece set, so it's only fair to put in a bit of care and maintenance in the interests of keeping it sweet.

LIVING WITH A WILLY

Getting it caught in things

The most common things to get your knob caught in are zips, photographs and girls.

There are boys who are clumsy with all these things. Me, I was an early casualty of the zip trap. One summer I was playing football in the garden with my mates. I rushed indoors to have a wee, but was keen to get back outside quick because I was on to a possible hat-trick. So I gave the winkle a quick shake, popped it back in my khaki shorts and whipped the zip up with one hand while the other was already on the door knob. Suddenly I was overcome with this terrible pain.

It was like someone had squeezed a thousand lemons, mixed them with a gallon of onion vinegar, scrubbed my face with a Brillo pad and dunked me into the brew. Every inch of my existence stung. A trillion stinging nettles called out my name. I could hear tightly stretched violin strings screeching in my ears.

I looked down and there it was, the sad little chipolata chomped between hard-edged, shiny steel zip teeth that seemed to scoff at the tenderness of my most intimate flesh.

I was paralysed. I couldn't move forwards or backwards. Breathing was painful. My hands only fluttered like sparrows round a bird table, never daring to alight on the trousers, for fear of inducing more of the searing pain that washed in great crashing waves over my body.

Any Other Business

At the very tender age of five, I had stood on the precipice of hell and looked down into the writhing pit of agony. It brings tears to my eyes even now to think back to that raw and torturous moment in my formative years.

Thankfully my dad came to my rescue on hearing my choked squeals and administered a steady hand and a tube of Savlon. I lived to tell the tale. I took great care with zips from that day forth. And I never ever got anything near scoring a hat-trick at football again. Possibly a world-class player was nipped in the bud.

Most men are little shy and embarrassed about their penises. Unless they are very confident and show-offy, most of us like to keep it covered. Even in sexy situations, there is a tendency to slip under the covers and wriggle out of your boxers rather than be brash about it.

There are others though, the ones who are desperately proud of how well hung they are, who like to parade around at any opportunity making sure the assembled company clocks the size of their todger. Usually this only ever happens in the changing room, where it's only other men who have to suffer the sight.

But there are some men who get sexually aroused by exposing themselves to women. 'Flashers' are often men who get a kick out of showing their dick to some female stranger. This sorry thrill usually comes about because they are unable to form proper relationships with women. They are sad cases who derive pleasure from sexual shocking. Often they are impotent men who are

147

unable even to get an erection when it comes to close contact.

Flashing, or exhibitionism, is a criminal offence that can carry a sentence of imprisonment for up to twelve months. The traditional haunt of flashers is parks, where they get a kick out of showing their tool to some unsuspecting passing female. Obviously this can be a very upsetting and frightening experience for any girl, although most of the time this sort of exhibitionist intends no real harm and doesn't want to touch or approach the person they're exposing themselves to. They are sick and sad men.

There's another sort of exhibitionism that goes on these days that is in some ways even more sick and sad. There's a type of lad who gets a big thrill out of getting drunk and taking his kit off to expose himself to the pub, club or coach full of fellow travellers.

And then there are the guys who have taken up the 'gangsta rap' habit of grabbing and tugging their crotch to emphasize a point of expression. All this willy clutching and flashing is sad, because it's also about a total inability to relate. Instead of being able to enter into a friendship and relationship that develops into sex, some boys can only short-cut to communicating with their willy. And it's not as though it's a prelude to sex, because for most of these lads who are whipping off their trousers down the rugby club in front of their mates and a few girls, it's instead of sex. They don't ever get past waving their dick about because they don't know how to communicate properly with girls.

7

Living with Your Willy

The willy can be a man's best friend; bring him endless fun, excitement and comfort. But it can also be his worst enemy. There are men who think with their willy all their lives and end up sad and lonely.

Most men's knobs are attracted to sex and sexy things, but this attraction doesn't equal a relationship. Some men have a series of one sexual partner after another, and as each one loses her allure they move on to the next. So all that ever exists between them is sex.

Sex is good at times, and very good occasionally, but its appeal doesn't last forever. What can last forever is friendship. Although your willy might lead you glans-first into sexy situations and compel you towards attractive girls, what is important is that you also form relationships.

Your willy is not the best judge of character – you are.

Don't let it rule your life: it's a useful and fun accessory. Look after it and it will look after you. By all means listen to it when it's not feeling well and get it checked out quick, but remember that there are also times to ignore it.

Your skin is your biggest sex organ and your brain the most powerful one. It's inside your brain that you'll find sensible answers to life's questions about love, lust and the universe, not inside your boxers.

The secret to a well willy is a well head.

Living With Your Willy
Useful Contacts

Brook Advisory Centres
Offer free and confidential sexual-health advice and
contraception to under-twenty-fives. Phone for details
of your nearest clinic or for urgent advice from 11 a.m.–
3 p.m Monday–Friday. Freephone 0808 802 1234.
www.brook.org.uk

ChildLine
A confidential twenty-four-hour phone line and website
for young people who want to talk about a problem with
a trained counsellor.
Freephone 0800 1111
www.childline.org.uk

Family Planning Association (FPA)
Provides information on all areas of sexual health and
can put you in touch with your nearest GUM clinic and
services. There is a special section for young people on
their website.
Helpline: 0845 122 8690. Open 9 a.m.–5 p.m.
Monday–Friday.
www.fpa.org.uk

askTheSite
A website that deals with many issues facing young
people, including sex and relationships. You can email
your questions to the site.
www.thesite.org

LIVING with a WILLY

GUM (Genito Urinary Medicine) or STI (Sexually Transmitted Infection) Clinics

There are clinics in most areas and at your local hospital. Ask the FPA (see above), your GP or call NHS Direct for details, on 0845 4647.
www.homehealth-uk.com/medical/gumclinics.htm

National Chlamydia Screening Programme

Contact for more information about chlamydia and testing.
Freephone 0800 567 123
www.chlamydiascreening.nhs.uk

National AIDS Helpline

Help and advice for those affected by HIV and AIDS.
www.avert.org

Terrence Higgins Trust

Charity that provides information on sexual health and HIV/AIDS issues.
Helpline 0845 122 1200
www.tht.org.uk